One Thousand Days in Siberia

Iwao Peter Sano

One Thousand Days
in Siberia

The Odyssey of a
Japanese-American POW

University of Nebraska Press
Lincoln and London

© 1997 by the University
of Nebraska Press
All rights reserved
Manufactured in the
United States of America

⊗ The paper in this book
meets the minimum requirements
of American National Standard
for Information Sciences —
Permanence of Paper
for Printed Library Materials,
ANSI Z39.48-1984.

Library of Congress
Cataloging-in-
Publication Data

Sano, Iwao Peter, 1924 –
One Thousand Days in Siberia:
the Odyssey of a Japanese-American
POW / Iwao Peter Sano.
p.   cm.
ISBN 0-8032-4262-X (cloth : alk. paper)
1. Sano, Iwao Peter, 1924–.
2. World War, 1939–1945—Personal
narratives, Japanese. 3. World War,
1939–1945—Personal narratives,
American. 4. World War, 1939–1945—
Japanese Americans.
5. Prisoners of war—Russia
(Federation)—Siberia—Biography.
I. Title.
D811.S3228 1997
940.54'8252—dc21
[B]   96 – 54629
CIP

Second Printing 1998

*To fellow prisoners who helped
me survive my days in Siberia*

Contents

Illustrations

Foreword

PATRICK SANO

As we grow older, our values of things in life keep changing. What were valuable to us in childhood are now trivial and even frivolous. Those things we held dear in our middle age now in our senior years are considered less important. But we hope the day never comes that we would see life's experiences as mere paltriness. We should see life as a series of sacred profanities.

This excerpt was taken from an entry in the third volume of my journal, which is presently being edited and compiled. It was written for a particular event that occurred in my life, but I discovered that it also has relevance to the kinship between my brother Iwao (the name by which he is known to members of our family) and me.

There is a custom in Japan known as *yooshi*. It means "a son to be nurtured." It is a custom by which a son of a relative or of a close friend is given up for adoption to a childless man and woman to be nurtured, to bear their name, and to inherit their birthright. Perhaps it is a practice that is also carried on in other cultures and by others as well, but I will write as best as memory serves me how it has affected our family.

This custom was the cause, and its effect, the writing of this book. Neither could Iwao have written it, nor would he have spent a thousand days in Siberia, had he not taken the role of *yooshi*. It was the mainspring.

On our maternal side, nine previous, consecutive generations had experienced famine in the way of childless rootstock. It was as if they had been persecuted by the gods, and consequently the lineage relied on *yooshi* to carry on its name. Its bloodline had "run dry" long ago, and on the back of many *yooshi*, the name persisted and was perpetuated.

After many years of discussion between my father and mother, the decision was made around 1937 that Iwao would be "a son to be nurtured" by Uncle Takakichi and Aunt Tsuya Suzuki in Japan, who were childless. Uncle Takakichi was the only remaining male Suzuki, and, without male progeny, that genealogy, if not its history, would terminate on his death.

It was a matter of family pride that my uncle and aunt were wealthy. Our family album contained photographs of their luxurious home, located high in the wooded hills above the village of Tomikawa. It was said that their home was constructed without a single nail, that it was fabricated and assembled with joints. It had all the modern plumbing conveniences, and its rooms were decorated with *byobu* (folding screens) flecked with gold dust! With a child's longing, Iwao and I gazed vicariously at those pictures over and over, feeling shortchanged that we lived in squalid shanties with neither electricity nor running water and had to use the outdoor privy.

Iwao, however, was destined to be delivered from these inconveniences, the crude housekeeping, and the personal regimen to become the future possessor of our uncle's wealth. As the eldest of three sons, I had always held the position "at the front of the line," but I was relegated to a role of rustic simplicity and austerity. I envied Iwao's good fortune, for his life henceforth would be that of an aristocrat, while I would remain a peasant. This was my immature appraisal of the situation then.

In the summer of 1939, Iwao left for Japan. After having said farewell to him, I helped my father prepare his field for the coming cantaloupe season. That summer, I witnessed my father in tears for the first time in my young life. He had endured much physical pain before without so much as a whimper or a complaint, but a wounded spirit caused him to weep. He found solace in weeping.

My father agonized over the decision he had made about Iwao. He had lost a son. He was torn between his love for his son and love for a childless couple. He forsook the nurturing of a begotten son; instead, he gave that love to a childless brother-in-law and his wife. My father chose Iwao as his gift of love. It was an Abrahamic act of sacrifice.

The sight of my father's tears marked a spiritual awakening for me, for I realized then that I had lost a brother. I felt ashamed that I valued wealth and the material conveniences so highly, unmindful of the fact that an irreplaceable kinship had been breached. Also, I realized then that my values were askew. I learned that human life, however modest or indigent, was more valuable than things, however ornate or priceless. I was taught the true priorities in life.

There is this simple proverb: "The deadliest foe to love is custom." My father and I met our foe in the custom *yooshi*; I believed at that moment that my father could have fought against custom, reneged on his promise, and taken back Iwao. But would that have released him from an aching spirit? The converse of this proverb is also true: the deadliest foe to custom is love. Despite the custom, my parents continued to pray for Iwao and his adopted parents. The Ultimate Love that was manifested to them in their prayers made the pain brought about by *yooshi* tolerable.

This is the broader ramification of Iwao's story. In a wider context, it is discovering family connectionalism in its peculiarities and idiosyncrasies. Emotions are at the heart of each meaningful experience of life. We are tied with one another, especially by those feelings aroused in enduring mutual hardships, and greater yet is the attachment when truths are discovered in pain and heartaches. Truly, it is of sacred profanities.

Finally, a look at Iwao's book itself. It is more than a collection of war stories, more than battles and skirmishes, destruction and annihilation of an external enemy. It is about an internal contention for self-determination, self-reliance, and self-realization. The ultimate sign of victory is not the peace treaty. Rather, it is the peace of mind, knowing he has tried his best to conquer himself. With his strengths, and despite his weaknesses, Iwao persists and in the end finds self-identity. He now knows what he is capable of doing, where he belongs, and who he is.

Iwao was not alone in his search. Indeed, his role as "a son to be nurtured" led his real parents and siblings to seek for their values and priorities. We were all involved in self-examination whether we could hold on to our faith and discern what is good despite unexpected and unusual vicissitudes of life.

Acknowledgments

After I returned to Japan from my two-year, nine-month exile in Siberia, the symptoms of malaria that I had contracted in that faraway land recurred twice. While lying on a futon to recuperate, I contemplated my future and decided that I must leave home to go to work. Although my adoptive parents expressed their desire that I resume my education, I somehow felt that it was necessary for me to strike out on my own.

In September 1948, three months after my repatriation to Japan, I left home for Kofu, the capital of Yamanashi Prefecture, to seek employment with the U.S. military government team there. Japan was, of course, under occupation by the Allied Forces then. I found a position as an interpreter-adviser for the information branch of the Civil Information and Education Section. In the fall of 1949, I was transferred to the Kanto Regional Office, located in Tokyo, where I joined the Information Section headed by Mr. William Giltner.

Mr. Giltner traveled extensively, accompanied by an interpreter, myself being one, in the prefectures under his jurisdiction to oversee the information activities of the local governments as well as community groups. It was on one of those field trips that he suggested to me in a casual sort of way that I write down whatever I remembered of my experience in Siberia, if for no other reason than leaving my story for my future family. I took his suggestion and began making notes.

The memories were fresh, and many pages were filled. I am deeply indebted to Mr. Giltner, who planted the idea in me. Without his urging, my Siberian experience would not even have been recorded.

I severed my ties with my adoptive parents and returned to America in 1952. The notes I wrote in Japan were put away and lay at the bottom of a desk drawer for a long time. I had, however, many occasions to share my experience verbally with my friends and acquaintances. Many of them felt that the story of my life in prison camp in the Soviet Union was a unique one and encouraged me to write a fuller account of it using my old notes.

Marylee MacDonald sat down with me with a tape-recorder and listened as I recorded what I remembered about the experience in as much detail as I could. Combining my old notes and the recorded account, she produced the first typed pages of the story. My writer friends added a great deal to improve the manuscript: Robert McAfee Brown, author of many books, suggested titles for the chapters that were far more enticing than the ones I had put on them originally; Gabrielle Rico went through the text with an eye of an English professor to suggest appropriate word and sentence changes; and Bill Hosokawa, former editor of a newspaper and a Nisei, raised many questions about sections of the story that were unclear or needed more explanation and shared with me his sensitive observations from the perspective of an Asian American. Bob and Sydney Brown, Tom James, Dan Okimoto, and the late Mildred Martin gave me many helpful and encouraging words. Elizabeth Plowman put the entire manuscript on a computer disk. James Gebhardt, reviewer of the manuscript, made valuable recommendations to improve the story. Jan Shuler and Nat Gorham, publishers of *Arabian Horse World*, helped with pre=press layout. My brother, Pat, sent me his thoughtful and candid feedback as a member of the family. Other friends and members of the family, too many to mention here, took the time to read the manuscript and encouraged me to pursue the possibility of putting the story in print. I must mention Minako, my wife, who added her own memories of the war days to my account, prodded me to keep working to complete the project when I failed to give enough time and attention to the task, and spent many hours editing and typing the text. To all of them, I owe a great deal.

Forty-eight years have elapsed since I left Siberia, and my memories of those years have grown ever dimmer. The memories of hardships and painful incidents, particularly, seem to have faded like a dream, and the sting is almost gone. Many of them are recalled even with humor. The only feeling that has grown a great deal of late is my gratitude toward those who did so much to help me through the harsh and trying days.

IWAO PETER SANO

Chronology

September: Germany invades Poland. World War II begins in Europe.	1939	June: Sano leaves United States to live in Japan as adopted son of his uncle and aunt.
December: Japan bombs Pearl Harbor. World War II begins in the Pacific.	1941	Sano resides in Tokyo as a high school student.
February: Roosevelt issues Executive Order 9066 to relocate people of Japanese ancestry on West Coast to internment camps inland.	1942	February: Sano's father in United States is taken by FBI to detention facility in North Dakota. May: The rest of the family is sent to Poston, Arizona.
July: Prime Minister Tojo's war cabinet falls.	1944	Sano returns to uncle's home from Tokyo to wait to be drafted.
August: Hiroshima and Nagasaki are destroyed by atomic bombs. Japan surrenders.	1945	March: Sano is drafted and sent to Manchuria. August: Sano is captured by the Soviets and sent to Siberia as POW.
May: Japan's New Constitution abolishing the military goes into effect.	1947	Sano works in a munitions factory, a collective farm, and coal mines in Siberia as POW.
Japan continues on the road to recovery from devastation of the war.	1948	June: Sano is repatriated to Japan and begins working for the Occupation.
April: Peace Treaty signed in San Francisco in 1951 goes into effect, ending the Allied Occupation officially.	1952	March: Sano leaves his adoptive parents and returns to United States.

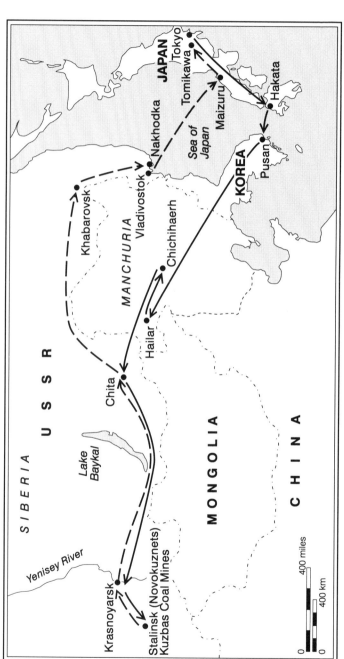

My Journey to Siberia and Back, 1945–1948

One Thousand Days in Siberia

1. Prisoners of the Russians: Destination Unknown

The gates of the huge military base had closed behind us. We were now prisoners of war, a rude awakening! I felt a sharp pain and a shiver in the pit of my stomach as we faced a future so bleak and uncertain. No Soviet soldier had guarded us until this moment. Late at night, we heard gunshots. Some Japanese soldiers had attempted to escape by climbing over the fence, I was told.

The Soviet soldiers were stationed as guards outside the gates of the base, which now was an assembly center for hundreds of Japanese soldiers gathering from all directions. How ironic, I thought, that Sergeant Yamamoto's superior, Lieutenant Sasaki, who had been sent to Tokyo six months before to escort us to Manchuria, was the very same commander who had led us down the Great Khingan Mountains to the train and finally right into this prison camp. "When was he aware of Japan's surrender?" I asked myself. Why did he continue to herd us, and why did we follow like sheep, without doubt or resistance, into this camp? It was obvious that this man took orders and followed them without giving much thought to the consequences, just as we, his subordinates, followed his orders.

It was some time later that I heard that the entire Kwantung Army stationed in Manchuria—one million troops—became captives of the Soviet Union without resistance, although it was rumored that some officers in command had debated whether to surrender immediately or do whatever they could to escape. It is puzzling that the surrender took place without any incidents of soldiers fighting to the end or even taking their own lives rather than being captured. The kamikaze missions are well known, and so is the account of the women and children who leaped to their deaths off a high cliff rather than surrender after the island of Saipan fell to the Americans. I believe that those of us in Manchuria simply obeyed an order from higher authorities without questioning, as all Japanese had always been trained to do. I was told later that people back in Japan accepted the surrender obediently and peacefully as the emperor went on the air on 15 August 1945 to plead with his subjects that they set aside the shame of surrender, swallow their pride, and accept peace for the sake of saving the country from further destruction.

The buildings we occupied were typical army barracks to which soldiers of the same squad were assigned together. For the next eight days we spent in Chichihaerh, we did little more than follow orders to do chores such as setting up meals and taking care of trash. Optimistic that we would be able to return to Japan soon, we simply waited, visited with one another, and slept.

We talked much about what we should have done the last few days or at least after we were ordered to surrender our weapons. One of the recruits, who had lived in Manchuria before entering the 118th Regiment, was simply mortified that we literally walked into this trap. He said repeatedly how we could have abandoned our uniforms and changed into civilian clothes, faded into the mass of refugees at some point, and continued our journey south and eventually back to Japan. How drastically different my experience would have been had that been the case!

As small groups began to leave the camp, rumor spread that those who left were going south to repair bridges and railroads damaged by the retreating Japanese military. Eventually, the rumor went, they would board a ship and return to Japan. On the eighth day, we received orders to prepare for departure. We were each to take with us the uniform we had on, an extra pair of underwear, a shirt, two pairs of socks, and a raincoat or a tent. Only a few men who were disabled or too ill to move were left behind. Farewells and greetings of "I'll see you back in Japan" were exchanged cheerfully, and we were off on what we all believed to be our journey home.

I was among the two thousand prisoners who went out the gates of the huge military base at Chichihaerh after eight days. There were young Soviet soldiers with machine guns, yet looking friendly and smiling, guarding us up and down both sides of the column as we were marched down the streets that warm mid-morning on the way to the railroad tracks.

A long line of boxcars was sitting along the spur tracks. As I passed the freight cars with their sliding doors open, I looked inside and saw that each car was divided into upper and lower decks with planks of wood. "This is what we'll be riding in to get home," said Sergeant Kondo, our squad leader. The men at the head of the column began climbing in, and soon I found myself among the thirty men in the eighteen-ton freight car allotted to our squad. The car was much too small for this number of people, but no one complained. I was not alone in thinking that we could put up with any discomfort or inconvenience for this next trip since we were going home at last. Half the group, mostly senior soldiers, climbed up to the upper deck, while the recruits occupied the floor level, just the way it was in the army barracks in Hailar. There was just enough space under the upper-level planks for us to stay in a sitting or squatting position, and if one wanted to stand up, one moved to the center of the car, where there was uninterrupted space from floor to ceiling. With the doors now closed, it was stifling hot inside the car. Later that afternoon, the train finally began to move. It suddenly stopped and then began to move forward again, but at a crawling pace. "Guess we're getting onto the main tracks," said Kondo.

The "passengers" were engaged in animated conversations and even in singing, as if to defy the undercurrent of tension they could not quell. The train soon was approaching the crossing where it would be switched onto the main line and where we would know whether we were headed north or south by the way the train made its turn. If it turned left, it would be heading south and home; if, God forbid, it turned to the right, it would mean that we were heading north and away from home. The prisoners strained to look out of each of the four small corner windows near the ceiling. "The great divide" was coming closer with each clicking of the wheels on the tracks. The train came to a halt. "How is it?" called a prisoner who was brave enough to ask, breaking the silence. "Can't tell yet," came the reply from another prisoner looking out the window. The seconds ticked by. The train jerked forward but stopped again. Then, with a second jerk, it began to move. "Hey! It's . . . it's . . . we're going north!" cried the man at the window. I felt as if everything were crumbling around me. "We're going north, north, north. . . ." The echo rang through my head. The train was now traveling at its normal speed, and the dim light of early evening came through the four open windows. No one was interested in looking out anymore. Weighed down by sorrow and helplessness, we sat in heavy silence.

It was Sergeant Kondo who finally suggested, "Hey, I'll bet we're going north to Hailar. They said there were some skirmishes up there—so I think we're going there to do some cleanup work." "Optimist," someone jeered back from the dark corner below. "Yeah?" retorted Kondo, who, as the highest-ranking noncom in the car, did not like back talk from a subordinate. "Why do you think they had so few Russian guards when we left the camp back at Chichihaerh coming to the station? They didn't give a damn if we tried to escape because we're going back to Japan anyway." Everyone fell into silence once more. I knew I wasn't alone in hoping Kondo would be right.

Before daybreak the next morning, the train passed through Hailar without stopping. The scenery beyond Hailar was new to all of us, although it was the same vast expanse of flatland dotted with small clusters of inhabited areas here and there. "Maybe we're going up to the border to do some work," someone else offered, sharing his wishful thinking. We soon came into Manzhouli, a town that sat on the border of Manchuria and Siberia. The train did not stop there, either. Kondo, now looking at a map spread on the upper deck, went on with his speculation that we were being taken to Chita, and then to Vladivostok, a port on the Sea of Japan. He reasoned that the Soviets were transporting us only through their own occupied territory instead of southern Manchuria and Korea. "Yeah, I'll bet that's right," everyone agreed.

The train did not travel steadily; sometimes it would stop for hours, and at other times it seemed to keep going for an entire day without stopping. When it came to a stop after such a long run, all the prisoners would jump out of the cars to relieve themselves. At the beginning of our journey, we would run some distance away from the train, trying to find a little privacy. As the days went by, however, we cared less and less about such privacy and answered nature's call right beside the train. The Soviet guards would then come along and poke at us with their rifles, gesturing for us to go farther away from the train. One of the guards frowned and mumbled something in Russian that we took to mean, by his gesture, that we were within view of some local women. In just a few days, the proud and elite Japanese soldiers were fast losing their dignity and self-respect.

The guards walking up and down beside the train while the train was at a station did so not merely to guard the prisoners. It appeared that they were more concerned with keeping the curious onlookers away from the train. Some of us tried to talk with the guards, using only a few words we thought they would understand. We asked, "Moscow?" pointing in the direction we thought Moscow would be, and then "Tokyo?" pointing in the opposite direction. The guard shook his head and walked away. He either didn't know or was not allowed to tell us our destination.

One night I was awakened by someone shouting, "It's the

ocean! It's the ocean! It's the Sea of Japan!" I climbed up on the upper deck and crawled over to one of the windows and pushed myself to the front. In the moonlight I saw a vast expanse of gleaming water extending far off to the horizon. It seemed as though the whole squad was trying to catch a glimpse of the water from the small windows. "Ah! I can even smell Japan," said Kondo. "See what I told you guys. What would the Russians want with us anyway? We never fought with them for more than a few days." Some of the more impatient prisoners said to one another eagerly, "I wonder how many days it'll take to get to Japan." "Maybe it was better coming this way. Now we can say we've even been to Russia."

The train came to a stop. The door opened, and everyone jumped out. Some prisoners went up to the Russian men and women standing nearby. Much incomprehensible babbling went back and forth between the Russians and the Japanese as the rest of us gathered around them. Out of all the exchange, someone soon picked out the word *Baykal.* "Hey, they say this is Lake Baykal." "What! Lake Baykal? Not the Sea of Japan?" "Who said this was the Sea of Japan? Could you smell any salt in the air?" said someone from another car. I dragged my feet back to the train from which I had so joyfully scrambled off only moments before. I felt as though I could barely lift myself back up into the car. "Where in hell are they taking us, anyway?" someone behind me asked angrily. The train resumed its irregular journey, and it seemed that we traveled along the shore of this huge body of water for two days before it was out of sight.

The long train with its two thousand bewildered prisoners continued its westward journey for several more days. We were, by then, dirty and smelly, but few cared about that; we were only aware of a nagging sense of hunger. Meals consisted mostly of food cooked Japanese style and were distributed via a couple of prisoners from each car, who were sent as carriers with lunch pails to fetch food for the whole squad. When the food was brought back to the car, dividing it equally was a painstaking task. All eyes were focused on the men in charge of this duty so that no one would get a bite more than anyone else. On occasion, when the stops were brief, the meal could not be picked up by the carriers before the train began to move. Since the train did not wait, we went without anything to eat until the next mealtime came along. We now spent the entire time between meals thinking and talking about food. People suddenly became experts on how to prepare various delicacies they had enjoyed back home. No longer did anyone seem ashamed of this preoccupation with eating, quite contrary to the old Japanese saying, "A warrior, even in hunger, must use his toothpick ostentatiously as if he has eaten his fill." In many ways, dignity for this band of "warriors" was fast vanishing.

Early one night the train came to a station where it was pushed back and forth for what seemed a very long period of time before it finally came to a halt. "I think we've arrived at our destination," said Kondo. "We'll probably leave the train tomorrow morning," he continued in his all-knowing way. I somehow managed to doze off.

It was the middle of the night. Ohta, who was sleeping on the floor near the door, suddenly yelled out, "Help! Help! Help me! Somebody's stealing my blanket!" The entire train was aroused by the commotion, and those who were sleeping near the door finally forced it shut and wired it closed from the inside. Next morning I heard that a Russian man with a knife had come into some of the cars, grabbed everything he could lay his hands on, and thrown it out on the ground outside. Several men and women were waiting to gather up the loot. They used the blanket they had taken first as a wrap for all the other items. It was a terrifying experience. We never imagined that prisoners would be robbed of their meager possessions.

The next morning, we all got off the train and formed a line outside. There were local people gathered around the tracks, looking at us with much interest. An officer admonished us, "Hey, you soldiers. Can't you look more lively? These Russians are going to make fun of you." "What's the difference? We are prisoners, aren't we?" mumbled the man standing next to me with a hint of disgust in his voice. As if trying to impress the townspeople gathered there, a young man who had just completed officers' training pulled out his long samurai sword from its sheath swiftly and smoothly and bellowed, "Attention!" The bystanders looked at this "show" in amusement, pointing their fingers at him, some smiling, and others even laughing.

We began our march from the station. Walking about half a mile, we came on our camp. It had not been newly constructed for our use, but by the strong smell of lime we knew that it had been given a fresh coat of whitewash. We were told by one of the officers that we were on the outskirts of a city called Krasnoyarsk. The camp was composed of seven rows of barracks. There were also five other structures within the high wooden fence with barbed wire strung along the top that encircled the camp. The five other buildings included two latrines, the mess, the warehouse, and the water station. At each corner of the compound, built as part of the fence, were four wooden towers where armed guards were posted.

The entrance to the camp was a large pair of gates swinging on hinges. It was wide enough for a truck to pass through. Each barracks building housed three hundred prisoners. Our straw mattresses were placed on wooden platforms, each large enough to accommodate twenty-four people, twelve on the lower level and twelve above. There were only half a dozen naked lightbulbs for the entire barracks. Dingy and gloomy, they did nothing to lift our spirits.

On higher ground, not too far away from the camp, was the city itself, which was built around a factory where we would be working soon. The huge factory, which included a foundry and shops for making wheels for trains, antiaircraft guns, and other weapons, was the lifeline of this Siberian city, providing work for most of the people who lived there. The Yenisey River was close by, and behind the camp was a plateau, which someone named "Krasnoyarsk Fuji," although it had no resemblance whatsoever to the magnificent mountain back home. There were no trees in or around the camp. The sloping landscape was barren and desolate. It was late September already, and the nights were cold. I lay down on the bunk, wide awake. I could not erase from my mind the sight of the high walls, the barbed wire, and the locked gates. How had this happened? From the sunny and open fields of southern California where I was born and raised as an American boy, I was sent to Japan a few years back to live a life that was so different from what I had known, so rigid and foreign. I had accepted that change rather stoically as my fate or a duty to my family. Wasn't that enough? But now this! It was unreal. I was angry, afraid, and depressed.

2. Back in America

I was born in 1924 in Brawley, California, a town located in the heart of Imperial Valley, near the Mexican border, the fifth child of Ichizo and Tsuta Sano, who had emigrated to the United States in the early 1900s. My father's birthplace is Shizuoka Prefecture, eighty miles southwest of Tokyo, the region known for Mount Fuji and excellent tea and the tangerines grown there. My father was twenty-one years old when he left Japan for America, arriving in 1905 aboard a freighter with a group of Japanese immigrants destined for Mexico. From Vera Cruz, where he landed, he traveled on foot toward Texas and after two years entered the United States.

Although small in stature, he was a man of extraordinary stamina and strong will. What I remember most about him are his spirit of independence, his willingness and courage to try new things and face new situations, and his great compassion for those less fortunate than he. Shortly before he turned twenty-three, he began life in America in the town of Imperial, as an alfalfa irrigator on a ranch, a job he found in a Japanese newspaper published in Los Angeles. After several months at this job, he received an offer to work on a cantaloupe farm that had been leased by another immigrant from Japan. The two men toiled day and night, and although their efforts ended in complete failure the first year, they succeeded in yielding great harvests of cantaloupes in subsequent years. My father saved whatever money he could out of his profits from this farm, and in 1909 he leased eighty acres of land in Brawley. He operated a successful dairy farm there, making him—my family claims—the first Japanese cowboy in America.

As was true with many young men who immigrated to America in those days, my father decided to take a trip back home when he was thirty-two to choose a bride with whom to share his life in America. Arrangements were made through relatives for him to meet a young woman from Tomikawa, Yamanashi Prefecture, a neighboring prefecture to his birthplace, Shizuoka. For Japanese women of my parents' generation, choosing their own suitors was usually out of the question. Their parents, relatives, and acquaintances started looking out for possible suitors long before they were of marrying age, taking into consideration compatibility in personality, age, the financial and social status of the families involved, education, and other factors. Tsuta Suzuki was then twenty-three years old, nine years younger than my father. They had not known each other before, but they were joined in marriage just as arranged. It was 1916. In those days, almost all marriages were arranged in this manner; arranged marriages still take place today, although the practice is increasingly less common.

Like my mother, many of the women who had married immigrants traveled five thousand miles across the ocean to live in America with husbands they had not known before. They accepted it as their fate and resolved to endure any hardships as pioneer women. Many had a dream of returning to Japan in a few years with the money saved from their hard work in America, known as a land of promise and opportunity.

In 1916, the newlyweds returned to America and immediately started a family. In two years' time, my brothers Yoshito and George were born on the Beatty Ranch in Brawley. The dairy farm had prospered and made my parents quite well off financially. They did so well in the dairy business that they soon out-grew the ranch, and my father proceeded to lease 160 acres west of Westmoreland to expand his business.

Then tragedy struck in the spring of 1918. Yoshito was a year and a half old at the time. My mother took him in a baby carriage to a pond near where the family's horse was grazing. Feeling the strong heat of the sun, she went back into the house to get her son's straw hat. As she came out, she saw the head of the horse beyond the bank of the pond. She climbed the bank hurriedly, only to find, to her horror, the baby carriage overturned and Yoshito floating face down in the water. She dashed to grab him, but he was already motionless. She surmised that the horse had accidentally knocked the carriage over into the pond.

As if losing their firstborn in such a tragic accident were not enough, George, their second child, met a terribly painful death. Shortly after the death of Yoshito, my mother was hospitalized in Los Angeles with a suspected case of tuberculosis. The diagnosis confirmed that she was tubercular, but her doctor felt that the desert climate in Imperial Valley would be good for her, and he therefore released her from the hospital on the condition that she spend as much time outdoors as possible. My father decided to leave George with a neighbor while he went to Los Angeles to bring his wife home.

George was about two years old. That day, the neighbor was using lye to make a processed vegetable called *kon-nyaku*, a root vegetable that immigrants from Japan had known and enjoyed eating back home. Thirsty, and not knowing that it was lye, little George drank the liquid from the glass, severely burning his throat and esophagus. He did not die immediately, living a few more agonizing years, years agonizing for my parents as well, as they watched him slowly lose his battle to live.

My mother was pregnant with a third child when the decision was made to take George to Japan to obtain medical care there, the doctors in the United States having given up hope and giving him no chance for recovery. George continued to suffer from the burn and needed to be hospitalized frequently while they were in Japan. He died after my mother returned to America with him. He was nearly five years old.

Yoneko, my sister, was born during my mother's stay in Japan. Because of George's severe condition, my mother was persuaded by relatives to leave baby Yoneko in care of her mother, as the day for her return to America approached. She, of course, intended to visit Japan again in a few years to bring Yoneko back to America. As events developed between Japan and the United States in the subsequent years, however, that plan never materialized. My mother visited Japan again in 1934 with my younger sister and brother and brought Yoneko, fourteen years old then, with her when she returned to this country in the hope that her daughter would be able to remain in America as a permanent resident. I can well imagine my father's excitement and happiness as he waited for the arrival of a daughter he had never seen before.

Born in Japan of a woman who was an "alien" in the United States, however, Yoneko was not an American citizen, and the government would not allow her to stay. Sympathetic and influential friends of the family, both Japanese and Caucasian, made great efforts to appeal the case before the immigration authorities, but to no avail. As a boy of twelve, sitting in a deep couch in the living room of Mr. Robinson's home, I saw my father tell his friend that his daughter was being sent back to Japan. Mr. Robinson asked in his loud, gruff voice, "What is the matter, doesn't Yoneko like this country?" As my father explained to him that it was the law that was forcing her back to Japan, Mr. Robinson's face suddenly turned red, and he began to curse in his customary colorful language the existence of such a law and the harshness of the immigration officials. Yoneko had no choice but to go back to Japan after less than two years of living with her parents, brothers, and sisters. My parents were heartbroken by the cruelty of a law that would not allow a child to live with her parents. Yoneko later married a man from a neighboring village and now lives in Tokyo with her two sons and four grandchildren.

Of the nine children my parents had, there was one more child besides Yoshito and George who died young. Ruth, a year younger than I, was a victim of spinal meningitis, which claimed her life overnight when she was two years old. I was too young to remember much about her. My parents must have gone through incredible grief and pain to have lost three children in such tragic ways. Besides Yoneko and the three who died young, I have an older brother, Patrick, two younger sisters, Florence and Belle, and a brother, Roy, the youngest of the family. All of them live in various regions of California.

My brother Pat and I had the normal share of sibling altercations, although we were close growing up. I vividly remember our fights, which usually ended up with both of us undoing something the other had done as a chore assigned by our parents. It was Pat's job to clean and maintain the tidiness of the bedroom we shared, while my chore was to take care of the chickens the family was raising. Furious at each other in a fight, I would go in the bedroom, mess up the beds Pat had made, and scatter things all over the room, while in retaliation Pat would go out and let the chickens out of the cages, which, of course, caused me to chase them frantically to put them back into the cages.

We were five children in all, but growing up I felt that there were two sets of children, with Pat and me in one set and our three younger siblings in the other. I was often put in charge of the younger ones while my parents were away at church meetings; as my mother used to say, I was kinder and did a better job of baby-sitting. Pat, on the other hand, was involved in sports and other activities with his friends and did not show much interest in, or patience with, his younger siblings.

Many family excursions and summers spent away from Brawley are still vivid in my memory. Sunday afternoons after church, my father often took us to the desert to hike, exploring mud pots and the region's other geological wonders. On one outing, I stepped on a nail, which caused an infection in my right foot. In great pain from the swollen foot, I was unable to sleep.

My father came into my room and asked if I wanted to go out with him to look at the stars. He was something of an amateur astronomer and knew a great deal about stars. He loved to go out and watch the shimmering stars in the huge uninterrupted expanse of indigo sky over Imperial Valley, where there were no trees or mountains to block the view, as he remembered they did in the small village in Japan where he grew up.

Because of the heat in the valley, we abandoned our home in Brawley soon after the Fourth of July holiday every year and spent the rest of the summer at a rented house at some southern California beach. Many people in the Japanese community in Brawley made a similar annual exodus out of the valley and often chose the same beach, such as San Pedro or San Diego. The adults visited with one another in the lazy afternoons, while the children spent endless happy hours playing games, fishing, and swimming together. A few hours in the morning, however, were set aside for church school, which my parents and their friends organized for their children and insisted on our attending.

My parents were devout Christians. Converted to the religion at the time of George's death, their activities centered around the church. We were not allowed to miss Sunday school, and my parents always observed an evening prayer time before retiring. After the decision was made that I would be sent to Japan to live with my uncle, who was not a Christian, my mother insisted that I study the Bible daily and rewarded me with extra allowance for my savings account. The daily dose of cod-liver oil she gave me was another expression of her earnest prayer that I stay strong and healthy to assume responsibility in my uncle's family.

My father was always willing to let the pastor of the church use our automobile for his trips out of town. My brother Pat and I did not share our father's generosity with "our" family car and let him know of our displeasure. Once my father agreed to let the youth group of the church use the automobile for their outing. That was a mistake; the boy who drove it got in an accident before the group even left town. Although we were extremely unhappy about the incident, I remember my father was philosophical, saying that he would do it again if the need arose.

Elementary schools in Brawley were segregated, with the white children and the children of Japanese immigrants going to one school and Mexican and black children attending another on the east side of town across the railroad tracks. The Japanese students made up less than 5 percent of the student body, and they chose their friends mostly from among their own, perhaps because their parents were good friends in most cases and because many of them went to school together on weekends—to the Japanese-language school on Saturdays and the Christian or Buddhist church on Sundays.

The Japanese immigrants' children in Imperial Valley spoke in English even among themselves. As far as I could observe, this was not always the case in some other areas. Many of them excelled academically and in sports, a typical trait of Japanese families, who impressed on their offspring the importance of excelling in everything they undertook. My mother often told us that we were mere guests in this country and that therefore we must watch our manners, look extra neat and tidy, and refrain from "making waves." However, there was a high school student who did not conduct himself in this typical passive manner. Angered by the word *Jap*, which appeared as his race on his driver's license, he visited the motor vehicle office and demanded that his race be spelled out fully or a period be place after Jap. We were all amazed that a Japanese would be assertive enough to make such a demand, and we admired his courage.

When I was in the sixth grade, I had a teacher who insisted that we all treat each other with fairness and without prejudice. One day there was an incident of a lost lunch. Almost immediately, a child of a migrant family from the Oklahoma dust bowl was blamed for the loss. The teacher was quick to gather us all and admonish us about treating someone unfairly without any proof of wrongdoing simply because that someone was a stranger and "different." This teacher's beliefs and teaching left a deep impression on me, and I recall her to this day with deep admiration and respect.

Anti-Japanese sentiment did not always surface, but we knew it was there. My mother was reluctant to spend the summer months in the San Diego area because there were more blatant signs and incidents of discrimination against the Japanese there. My father once went to San Diego with the pastor of our church, Reverend Kuwano, to attend a church conference. On his return home, an FBI agent showed up at the front door. He asked if my father had visited San Diego and stopped by a dam on his way home. My father replied that he had. The agent further asked him what he was measuring and looking at with a set of binoculars at the dam. My father told him that he had visited the dam only to enjoy the view and have lunch. Puzzled and surprised by this man's knowledge of his movements, my father asked him how he knew about his trip. The man just smiled and left without giving him an answer.

One Sunday the *Los Angeles Examiner* printed an article attempting to alarm the citizenry with a scenario of possible Japanese bombings of targets in California should a war break out between the two countries. Reports of this kind so disturbed and worried people in the Japanese community that they began to talk about boycotting the Hearst papers. As a youngster, I recall seeing WHITE TRADE ONLY signs in some towns. Some of my Japanese-American friends, I was told, were not allowed to go into certain movie theaters. One of the derogatory remarks made by white people that I personally heard was from a girl at school who called soy sauce "bug juice," implying that the dark sauce was not fit for human consumption but only for the barbaric Japanese. I felt ashamed of who I was, which led me to write a report describing my meals as very much like anyone else's; I did not mention rice or fish.

During my last two years in the United States, I had a close

friend named Leonard, a Caucasian boy who lived in my neighborhood. We often visited each other's houses to do our home-
work and occasionally went to the Saturday matinee movies
together. In the spring of 1939, when Japan was into the third
year of war against China and newspapers reported a border incident flaring up in northern Manchuria between the Soviet Union
and Japan, Leonard said to me out of the blue, "Boy, you guys
are going to get it now! The Russians are really going to beat you
guys!" Looking back today, although I was his friend, I was not
a complete American in Leonard's eyes in spite of my American
citizenship by birth.

It has always been extremely important for people in Japan to
have their family names perpetuated from one generation to
another. An adoption was arranged if a family did not produce a
child to carry the family name to the next generation. If the children were all females, one of them took a husband who moved
in with the family and took the wife's family name. After my
mother visited her relatives in Japan in 1934, my parents decided to send one of the male Sano children to Japan to be adopted by her brother, who was childless. My brother Pat could not
be the one to go since he was the oldest male child and was
expected to carry on the Sano name, nor could it be Roy, who,
my parents had decided at his birth, was to become a minister in
the Christian Church. I was the one. I would be sent to Japan to
become my uncle's adopted son.

People often ask me how I felt about being chosen to leave
my own family and live permanently in Japan, simply to conform
to an old tradition. I can only say that I didn't give it a second
thought. My parents chose, and I simply accepted the decision.
It seems odd to me now that I didn't object or protest, but it
would not be true to suggest that I even questioned the decision,
let alone objected. Consequently, in the summer of 1939, I bade
farewell to my family and friends and left for Japan on a trans-
Pacific steamer. I was fifteen years old. I was to learn the Japanese
language, of which I knew very little, take up the family name of

my adopted father, Suzuki, and live the rest of my life in a culture that was unfamiliar to me, a teenage boy born and raised in America. As an adult and a parent myself now, I can imagine how difficult it must have been for my parents to give away one of their children. Even now, I can see their waving hands as they watched the steamship *Asama-maru* pull slowly away from the Los Angeles pier, cutting and dropping the colorful paper streamers into the water below.

There were a number of Nisei (Japanese-American) passengers aboard the *Asama-maru*, a few of them my age and others older. Some of the older ones had completed their college education but were unable to find employment commensurate with the training they had. They made a decision, therefore, to move to Japan to see if they could start anew and find better opportunities there. Still others had completed their high school education and had heard that even the college-educated Nisei had no choice but to work in the produce markets or as gardeners. They knew they could not afford to spend the time or the money to continue going to school when the prospect of jobs seemed so bleak. The doors of the work world were not open to young people of Japanese descent.

For the most part, however, we were in a happy mood, as if this were a vacation, even though, in the back of our minds, we were aware of what was awaiting us; we would have to learn everything from scratch, including the Japanese language, which we would have to be able to read, write, and speak for day-to-day survival.

When the *Asama-maru* docked at Honolulu, we were given time to go ashore and explore some sights. I spent the day with a boy my age named Johnny who was moving to Japan with his parents. After visiting some well-known tourist spots, we returned to the dock area. Looking up at the clock atop the Aloha Tower, Johnny said, "We still have time. Let's just lie here on the grass and enjoy this freedom. It won't be like this when we get to Japan." "What do you mean?" I asked. "Look, weren't you warned? There won't be dating, parties, movies, or things like that anymore," he answered. Yes, I was told of these things before, but suddenly a whiff of anxiety came over me as I lay there, listening to Johnny and looking up into the blue sky through the palm branches.

The steamship left the pier and was heading out of the harbor. We threw coins in the waters below as the local swimmers yelled to us, urging us to throw more. The sea was clear and deep blue.

3. Arriving on Japanese Shores

The steamship was approaching a pier in the harbor of Yokohama, one of the major port cities of Japan. The water below looked dark and muddy. There were tugboats towing three or four barges each, which, I was told, were night soil barges. Presently, the immigration officials came on board, and we were all assembled on deck. The officials with white gloves came down the line in front of us. One of the Nisei had a Leica camera with him and was directed to follow one of the officials to pay duties on it. Another of the Nisei was ordered to hand over a book in his possession to the customs authorities; it was returned to him immediately, but with several pages removed with a razor blade.

As I walked down the gangplank, my adoptive parents and my sister Yoneko spotted me quickly and rushed to meet me. I remembered my mother back in America telling me never to call my new mother and father *Aunt* and *Uncle* when I first met them, or it would be very difficult to correct myself afterward. My aunt, who was to be my mother, was sobbing and said in a teary voice, "We're so glad you're here; we have been waiting for so long." My uncle was standing some distance away from us. At the hotel where we were to stay overnight, we were served tea and a cold Japanese cider drink. My uncle, although sitting in the same room, was almost facing the other way. I was to learn later that the Japanese male did not allow himself to show his emotions whether the occasion was a joyous or a sad one, and my uncle was trying hard to hide what he was feeling from those of us who were with him.

We left Yokohama the next day and traveled to my Japanese home in Yamanashi Prefecture by train. What a surprise! Everyone was Japanese, and everyone spoke Japanese! I could understand at best only half of what was being said around me. I was told that I was to go and visit my relatives who lived in the area, accompanied by my aunt. These visits took a week to complete. I sat on the tatami (straw mat) floor and felt awkward and uncomfortable as the aunts, uncles, cousins, and others would bow their heads low, almost touching the floor. They served green tea wherever I went. I knew that people in the Japanese community back in America drank green tea, but it was a foreign drink to me up to this point. I was willing to sip it when it cooled off a bit. I tried hard to be Japanese. I even bowed my head as I said "Thank you" and "Good-bye."

It was summer, and the village children who were home on vacation stared at me with much curiosity. My father had engaged a tutor to come six days a week to teach me Japanese at home, and the lessons started a week after I got there. The teacher arrived at 7:00 A.M. and stayed until 1:00 P.M. He and my family decided that I would start with a first-grade reader, literally beginning with the ABCs of Japanese. Afternoon hours were spent reviewing and preparing for the next day. Such home instruction continued through the end of December 1939.

Arrangements had been made for me to go to Tokyo to prepare for enrollment in a high school there. In January 1940, accompanied by my parents, I left for Tokyo to live with the family of a Buddhist priest who taught Japanese at the high school. After a few months of intensive preparatory study, I entered the second-year class at the five-year high school. I was two years older than my classmates.

By this time, I was doing quite well with my daily conversation and was able to read and write in Japanese. Needless to say,

English class was no problem, and math was simply a review of what I had studied in California. On the other hand, military training was something completely new. In the first session, I was ordered by the officer/instructor to stand in front of the assembled class and given the commands for right turn, left turn, forward march, and halt. It was a disaster, causing my classmates to break into a chorus of laughter. I was called over by the officer, who said, "What the hell's wrong with you? Haven't you had any military training before?" "No, I'm Suzuki, and came from America," I replied. "Oh, so you're the one from America. OK, stand over there and watch today." Things were just as Johnny predicted when we were savoring moments of freedom in the grassy area by the Honolulu Harbor.

On Sunday, 7 December 1941 (Monday, 8 December, Tokyo time), the English teacher called me in to the faculty room. "Your parents are in America, aren't they? I'm sure they'll be OK. I was once a student at Washington State. I know Americans. They will treat your parents and siblings right," he said. Somehow, I was not that concerned about my family in America at the time and wondered why this teacher was trying to console me and relieve me of any anxiety I might have had.

I was still in Tokyo when sixteen B-25 bombers led by James Doolittle made the first attack on the city from the deck of the USS *Hornet*, an American aircraft carrier. It was 18 April 1942. I was to learn later that the tide of the war began to turn against Japan only a few months after that air raid.

I was accepted by a college in my fourth year of high school, but I forfeited the opportunity, gambling that I could enter my first-choice college if I studied another year in high school. How was I to know then that the military service exemption for liberal arts majors was to be canceled during my fifth year of high school? I gave up the idea of going to college and returned to Yamanashi to help on my sister's family farm in the absence of her husband, who had been drafted by the army earlier. There I awaited my draft notice.

In the spring and summer months, Mount Fuji was a deep, misty purple, soaring high above and beyond the green hills and lower mountains surrounding the village of Tomikawa in Yamanashi Prefecture. The villagers seemed to take Mount Fuji for granted. Having it in their backyard was a source of great pleasure and pride to them, and, although they were in awe—as anyone would be—of this splendid wonder with its sweeping, graceful slopes reaching the valley floor miles beyond the village borders, this world-famous mountain was simply a part of their lives.

It was the winter of 1945, late February. I stood behind my house and wondered if this might be the last time I would see the mountain with my own eyes. I would be back, for sure, but perhaps as little more than ashes in an unpainted wooden box, like those who had already been killed in combat and been returned to the village in the boxes wrapped in white cloth. I remember lining up with other village people as the boxes were carried back by fellow soldiers wearing white gloves.

The mountain seemed so close; it was snowcapped and every bit as beautiful as the photograph my father treasured and hung in our living room back in America. The mountain top glistened like crystal in the cold sky. I thought about a disturbing remark a neighbor had made not long ago. There was fear among some villagers, he said, that the mountain was being used by the B-29 bombers as a convenient landmark to locate Tokyo on their bombing runs. There had been numerous reports of bombings from many parts of the country since November.

My draft notice had arrived a month before. I was to report to the Twelfth Regiment in Tokyo on 1 March. Finally, my turn had come. Several young men of the village had been called and gone to war some months ago, and the fact that they had been drafted kept me wondering why I was still home. Could I have been overlooked by some freak clerical error?

An elderly man in the village, who often had interesting stories to tell, mentioned the case of a healthy young man who had awaited his draft notice for a long time. The people in the village began to gossip about him and spread rumors that perhaps he was avoiding the draft by claiming to be mentally retarded or that he had a social disease that caused him to be rejected after his physical. The young man felt so burdened by such talk that he finally visited the district draft office to look into the matter. There he found, to his surprise, that his name was listed on the last line of the page and that the book had been bound in such a way that his name had been folded into the binding. His inquiry led the authorities to force the book open to discover this error. To the young man's dismay, he was drafted immediately.

I had passed the physical with excellent marks, and I knew that I was healthy and strong, fit to be a model soldier on any battlefield. World War II was in its fourth year, and the press and radio continued to headline the victories of the Japanese military in the South Pacific. I eagerly waited for the day I would be drafted to serve my country. Eagerly? Perhaps. Was my feeling one of true patriotism or a sense of duty, knowing that I had no other choice in the matter? Memories of my days in California swept through my mind. What are my old friends at school and church doing now? I would be fighting against them this time. My parents must be worried and agonizing about my being here, knowing that I am of draftable age. I felt pain and wished that things were different. I also knew, however, that I had become a true Japanese in a very short time. I felt a strong sense of loyalty to Japan, or perhaps I simply acquiesced to the situation in which I found myself. After all, all Japanese were being called to make concerted efforts and even sacrifice their lives to ensure Japan's victory. We took seriously the government propaganda slogan, "We shall not ask for anything until victory is ours!"

Women tended the home front after the men of draftable age were sent to battle: there were children to look after, farms to manage, long queues to stand in to receive rationed food, letters to write to husbands and brothers on the faraway battlefields, and, most of all, there was morale to maintain in the face of the increasing hardships of day-to-day living.

People in the village have always had gatherings of relatives, friends, and neighbors for celebrations of births, marriages, anniversaries, and the completion of a new house and for mourning, too. Whatever the occasion, they gathered to feast and be together. A farewell party in my honor was planned. I was unaccustomed to large gatherings and rather shy about being the center of attention. More than once I told my adoptive mother of my reluctance to be the center of attention at such a party, but I was unable to dissuade her. She insisted that it was important to go ahead with the plan, especially because I was adopted. If she did not have a party, she said, the village people would gossip and say that it was because I was only an adopted son.

The house was crowded that evening with guests who gathered for the farewell party. This party was much like the others, with animated conversation and bursts of laughter. It was surprising that everyone had more than enough to eat and drink; the food shortage had become severe even in this farming community. The kinds of food suitable to serve at parties had long been unavailable, I thought. Raised in a traditional Methodist family, I had not tasted sake (rice wine) before and was reluctant to try it now, although the guests did their best to persuade me. I did not want to spoil the party by refusing and decided to empty the sake into my empty soup bowl as unobtrusively as possible. I hoped that no one was watching me do this, but I could not escape the watchful eyes of an uncle, who sat next to me. "What are you doing, Iwao? You're not going to let this good stuff go to waste, are you?" he whispered. He was more than willing to gulp down the sake in the soup bowl each time it was filled.

Early the next morning, I was ready to leave for Tokyo to report for duty but felt somewhat restless. Soon people would arrive to say their good-byes, deliver their good wishes and words of encouragement. Two women came to the door in the uniform of the Japan National Defense Women's League, a freshly washed white apron and a sash that draped from the left shoulder across the chest to the right side of the waist, on which was written in bold letters the name of the group. One of them said, "Take good care of yourself. We'll be praying for you so you'll be back safe." I thanked her and assured her I'd be all right. The relatives who had attended the party arrived. "Iwao, stay well. We know you'll be a strong and brave soldier," said an aunt. More neighbors and schoolchildren joined us and were served a cup of sake or tea with which to drink a farewell toast to me.

Three men from the Veterans Association arrived in their khaki uniforms. This signified that it was time for everyone to line up behind them for a procession to the neighborhood shrine. The village people had gone through this ritual repeatedly in recent months and were accustomed to the practice. I looked back at the house, wondering if I'd ever come back to live in it again. It stood serenely, out of step with the wartime uncertainties and turmoil we were going through.

We began our walk to the shrine singing patriotic songs everybody knew by heart: "I'll be back a victor, as I go gallantly off to battle. . . ." It had been an unusually cold winter, but the narrow path that led to the shrine from the house was cleared of the snow that had fallen several days before. The sun had not yet melted the hard frozen surface of the road to make it slushy. The paddy field stretching out on one side of the path in its winter rest was covered with a thin layer of ice. The procession halted in front of the *torii*, the shrine gate, and I was to leave the group there and go through the gate to approach the main structure of the shrine accompanied by only one of the veteran soldiers. It was customary for a departing soldier to visit a shrine to pray for victory for Japan as well as for his personal safety and health.

Praying and bowing in the Japanese style were not things I did with ease. I recalled the first time I had visited the imperial palace in Tokyo with a friend with whom I had grown up in Imperial Valley. It was soon after I had arrived in Japan. I was to bow low toward the palace as all Japanese would do, but I was extremely uncomfortable and therefore reluctant to do this. My friend whispered to me that it was not up to me to decide whether to bow: all Japanese were expected to pay respect to the emperor in this manner. Suddenly I was aware of the policeman in white gloves standing on duty nearby. For a fleeting moment I recalled standing up to salute the American flag each morning at school when I was a child, which, after all, might not be too different from bowing toward the imperial palace.

I don't remember what I prayed for at the shrine. I remember being more conscious of the people outside the *torii* waiting for me to finish the ritual, and it seemed more important for me to return to them as quickly as possible than to take time for prayers. I thought about the *haramaki* (a wide cloth band worn around the waist for warmth) and a good-luck charm my mother had given me. The *haramaki* was made of a piece of cloth called *sen-nin-bari*, which literally translated means "one thousand stitches," and many women of the village had sewn on it as a way of wishing me well. My mother was particularly pleased that she had a chance to place as many stitches as her age on the *haramaki* for her own son. All women who were born in a year of the tiger were believed to have extra strength and power to protect others from harm and therefore were asked to sew as many stitches as they were years old on the *sen-nin-bari*. Other women were allowed only one stitch each. Because she was born in a year of the tiger, my mother was asked countless times to sew those stitches for departing soldiers for good luck.

The narrow path we had walked to the shrine suddenly widened into a gravel road used for automobile traffic. The procession soon reached the village office, where I was joined by three other recruits from the village. There was an official ceremony planned for us in front of the office. The ceremony consisted mainly of speeches, first by the village mayor, followed by representatives of various patriotic citizens' groups and the recruits themselves. My father advised me to keep my speech

short. He warned me against exaggerations and empty promises. He had heard many draftees give long and brave speeches about how they would fight for the country, for the emperor, kill all enemies they encountered to revenge the B-29 bombings, and so on. I did make my speech short; all I wanted to do was to thank the people for coming out to see me off. It was now time for most people, including the schoolchildren, to bid farewell, leaving only a small band of relatives and close friends with me.

We proceeded to the rocky shore of the Fuji River, where we boarded a small wooden ferry to cross the river. I felt a chill in the air, although the sunshine enveloped everything around us. The river was so clear that every stone at the bottom could be seen through the gentle ripples. As I gazed down into the clear water, my thoughts wandered back to Imperial Valley, California, where I was born and grew up. Strangely, the clear water of this river had always reminded me of the muddy brown water of the irrigation canals in Brawley, which were fed by the Colorado River.

The ferry reached the other side of the Fuji River, and we began to walk the steep path up the cliff to the train station. Looking down, I saw the river bathed in the golden morning sun, the river that had become a strong link between my younger days in America and my life here in Japan. The four of us waited for the train that would take us to Kofu, capital of Yamanashi Prefecture, to join other draftees headed for Tokyo. Soon the train rounded the bend and came into the small Ide Station. The four of us, together with other passengers, boarded the train. We leaned out the train window and waved our arms in response to the cheers of *Banzai, Banzai!* (Long live the emperor!) as the train slowly jerked forward, rounded another bend, and disappeared into a tunnel.

At several other stations a few more recruits came aboard. I had the strange sensation that I was just watching this human drama in a country at war with a certain amount of detachment, as if I were a complete outsider, a mere spectator.

4. Assignment: Northern Manchuria

The train we boarded at Kofu sped into Tokyo, the big city I had not seen for nearly a year. Although Tokyo had not yet been the target of large-scale bombing, it was evident that a number of sporadic air raids had taken place as I saw destroyed buildings and leveled lots slip past the train window. The gutted buildings with black and broken windows stood like ghosts. There were gray piles of what must have been pieces of furniture and bedding. Where did the occupants of these houses go? Do they have relatives in remote villages? How do they make a new start with their homes and possessions destroyed? I only hoped the survivors were getting by somehow, somewhere, away from threats of destruction. The train pulled into Shibuya Station in the western part of Tokyo, where we got off and began our walk to the Twelfth Regiment in Setagaya Ward. The people on the street seemed different from what I remembered. They were like stray dogs wandering about aimlessly or trying to run away from something hostile. I wondered if these people were having sleepless nights from the frequent air-raid sirens or were simply tired from strenuous daily living in a country at war. I did not have time to pay too much attention to these changes, however. I was acutely aware that the time was drawing near when I was to enter the gate of the Twelfth Regiment barracks as instructed by the draft notice. It was 1:00 P.M., 1 March 1945.

Walking through the gates of the regiment, I felt as if I were being taken to prison. It was a totally different world, one from which I could not walk out. The seven days that followed at the regiment went by swiftly. We received injections and medical examinations while we were there, but there was no military training. This place was merely an assembly point, and soon rumor began to spread that we were to be sent overseas, where our combat training was to begin.

Actually, the possibility of an overseas assignment pleased us because, for one thing, there was a severe food shortage in Tokyo. One of the few times we were ordered into the bomb shelter, I heard a soldier chewing on the horse feed he had stolen from the stable. He was still very hungry even after a meal. I was about to throw away a bit of rice I had left in the dish before washing it. I was stopped just in time by a soldier who grabbed the rice out of my bowl with his hands and ate it quickly. The draftees from cities where rationed staple food had never filled their stomachs were perpetually hungry, while those of us who had lived in the farming areas still did not know what it was like to be acutely hungry.

There were B-29 air raids during the night. As the warning siren blared the first night, Sergeant Yamamoto, a tall man with pink cheeks, who had been sent from the overseas regiment to take charge of us, yelled, "Get everybody up, and go immediately to the shelters." The draftees from Tokyo, however, were so accustomed to air raids that they were able to tell by the sound of the planes whether the danger had passed. If the planes were already over-head, they told us, the bombs they dropped would fall beyond us. They would say, "Don't worry. It's safe now. For the bombs to land on us, the planes would have to be coming at us." They also claimed that they were able to detect where the bombs would fall by the whistling sound. Sergeant Pink-cheek quickly learned that it was hopeless to wake us up in the middle of the night after that and seemed to accept it good-humoredly. He was young and handsome and joked around with the brand-new soldiers. Not a typical mean army man, I thought to myself, relieved.

Although the 150 recruits in our group did very little while waiting for the day of our departure, we watched others who had arrived before us undergo training. One interesting exercise involved a tank made of cardboard. The young soldiers practiced throwing hand grenades at this "tank." The mock grenade was tied to a bamboo pole, which the men grabbed and went through the motion of casting at the tank. The officers and Sergeant Pink-cheek stressed that the training we would receive overseas would be nothing like these drills. We would be given a box of sand (in place of explosive powder) with which we would practice diving under a tank. In an encounter with enemy tanks, we would be ordered to carry a box filled with TNT and dive under an enemy tank.

The prospect of my becoming a human bomb in this manner did not frighten me much, as strange as it may sound. This kind of self-sacrifice, often called the Kamikaze Way, was not a notion foreign to soldiers or even to an average citizen then. From childhood, the Japanese were taught that it is a great honor, indeed a duty, to sacrifice oneself for the sake of the emperor and the country. In an elementary school textbook, there was a story of three soldiers who, during an earlier campaign in China, willingly carried a bomb into a barbed-wire entanglement to blow it up, and themselves with it, to create a hole through which other soldiers could run to attack the enemy. This was presented to children as the model of an exemplary and honorable act that any and all Japanese were expected to follow. I recall a song often broadcast on the radio, extolling soldiers who gave their lives in battle and sailors who died at sea without any regret. I, too, swallowed the whole notion without question.

The only kind of orientation that we received while we were at the Twelfth Regiment was reading a handbook called *Senjin-Kun*, a military manual that all soldiers were to obey. The rumor that we were bound for somewhere north was soon confirmed by the uniforms issued to us, heavy and warm for the winter season. Still, there was no official word as to where we were going.

A week later we received the order to leave the Twelfth Regiment, and we headed for the same train station that marked our arrival a week before. As we walked out the gate of the regiment, I was keenly aware of one fact: I was part of the military now, no longer just a young man walking the streets of the civilian world. The train took us to Shinagawa Station in the southern section of Tokyo, where we were transferred to a military train heading south on the Tokaido Line, the main trunk line connecting Tokyo to the southwestern part of Japan. This was the route I had often taken to go home to Yamanashi Prefecture from school in Tokyo for the summer vacation. I remember feeling disappointed to see Mount Fuji so bare and brown then, nothing like the picture of it we had in America. This time, however, the snowcapped mountain looked stunning and majestic, just like I wanted to remember it.

The train was too crowded even to take a nap. Men were trying to sleep on the floor as well as in the luggage rack above the seats. The train came to a sudden halt somewhere in Shizuoka Prefecture, as, we were told, several U.S. Navy Grumman planes flew overhead. A train in motion would be an easy target for the enemy planes, we were informed. Traveling along the beautiful Inland Sea a few hours later, we were told to close all the window shades for security reasons. I heard there were fortifications along the shorelines to prepare for imminent landing by enemy troops, but, of course, we did not see them with the shades down. I could not understand why we, as soldiers, were not allowed to see them.

The train continued its journey south and arrived at Hakata Station, Kyushu. There we were taken to a hotel to spend the night. We slept in twos on the quilted mattresses not much larger than sitting cushions. Imai, who was from Tokyo and shared a mattress with me, sighed, "This'll be the last night we can sleep on quilts. They'll put us in blankets next time we lie down. . . ." He went on mumbling that for the first-year soldiers this would be the last time to experience an erection, implying that life in the army would be too rigorous and exhausting to even think about sex. The lights were turned off. The drizzle outside turned to rain.

The rain had stopped sometime during the night; the morning sky was gray with the low clouds hanging over land and sea, which did not help our heavy hearts. Boarding the troop transport, we saw no one but the dockworkers, who did not bother to look up to see us. The image of children with red cheeks waving small flags and townspeople waving their hands and shouting their greetings back home flashed through my mind. Although I didn't realize it at the time, Japan was already in a state of exhaustion. People had little energy or vitality left, not to mention material supplies, from months and years of austere living. They no longer cared much about anything or anybody. What a contrast to the pier of San Pedro, California, where we spent our carefree summer days, swimming, fishing, laughing, and telling stories with friends!

It began to rain heavily again; the sea was dark and rough. The ship swayed and was tossed about violently by the high, foamy waves crashing against its sides. I went below once but was soon out on the deck again. I wanted to see as much of the land as possible so I could keep it in my memory. I had a feeling it might be a long time before I could see Japan again, if at all. The shores gradually sank from sight, and the rain was coming down in sheets.

At noon Sergeant Pink-cheek, who was taking us to his regiment in Manchuria, bellowed, "Lunch! It's lunchtime. Any of you who think your belly can take it go get your lunch on the deck above!" He was not much older than I or the rest of us. One of his duties was to educate us in the ABCs of life in the army before we got to our destination. Jokingly he would say, "You guys who got more education, better watch it when you get over there. Schooling won't count much where you're going."

With the sea so rough, few escaped seasickness. I was lucky. I enjoyed not only my own lunch but someone else's as well. People were scattered, groaning, all over the boat. The urine in the toilets was spilling over and flowing down onto the floor where the sick men lay helplessly. I heard someone say, however, that we were fortunate to cross the channel in this kind of weather. Were it calm, we could have been an easy target for the American submarines in the Sea of Japan ready to attack any Japanese ships that moved. They could have sunk our ship with torpedoes. I stood out on the deck and savored the cold air. Later I heard we were one of the last army transports to cross the Sea of Japan. We were the very last group of soldiers that Japan recruited. Perhaps no more young men were available for the draft at the point, or the military was aware that Japan was at its last gasp.

At dusk we arrived at Pusan, Korea. Korean women in their high-waisted blouses and long skirts made me realize that I was no longer on the mainland of Japan. Their chattering, too, entered my ears as something foreign. A group of small Korean boys dashed by, talking in Korean, of course. Sergeant Pink-cheek, pointing his thumb over his shoulder at them, said, "There are some Japanese who'll give those young rascals hell for using that language." (Korea was under Japan's domination at that time, and the use of the native language was officially forbidden.) For supper we were taken to a local grammar school. It took us twenty minutes to get to the school, ten minutes to finish our meal, and another twenty minutes to walk back to the dock. Amused, I thought to myself, "Is this efficiency? Is this the army way?"

After sunset we boarded the train moving north up the Korean Peninsula. As the train traveled through Korea, it avoided passing through the larger cities by day, perhaps for security reasons. Someone mentioned that the military did not want its soldiers to be seen being transported to Manchuria.

Japan had always been on guard against the Soviet Union as a potential enemy, and, for that reason, the one million soldiers of the Kwantung Army had been sent to defend Manchuria. When we arrived at our destination, we soon learned that the army was equipped with pitifully little hardware at that stage of World War II. We had been told back in Tokyo that our regiment was a heavy artillery unit, yet we soon found that there were very few cannons and guns. By then, most of the weapons that Japan possessed had been sent to the South Pacific, where the actual fighting was taking place, and the country was able to provide the northern defense force with few fighting tools. There was an army air corps, but it had no airplanes. As we headed north, Sergeant Pink-cheek informed us that Japan would now have to fight alone as Germany was going to surrender any day and Italy had already collapsed.

The train continued its course northward; the weather steadily grew colder. We crossed the Yalu River, which divided Korea from Manchuria, another reminder that I was going farther and farther away from my homeland. Looking out the double-paned window of the train, I saw the snow-covered land of Manchuria stretch all the way to the horizon.

On 15 March, the train finally arrived at its last stop, Hailar in northern Manchuria, some one hundred miles from the Soviet border. It was bitterly cold, with gray fog hiding the sun, and as I stepped out of the train my feet in my thin canvas shoes felt as if I were standing barefoot on ice. We stomped our feet, put up our collars, and pulled down the flaps on our headgear to cover our ears. "Turn up your ear covers! Hey, you over there, quit stomping your feet, and get in line. You! Where in hell's your hands, get them out of your pocket!" barked old Lieutenant Sasaki, Sergeant Pink-cheek's superior.

Hailar was a military town, consisting largely of the military compounds. The flatland stretched far into the distant hills, where, we were told, many fortresses were located. Later we were to find that every day was like a weekend for the little town of Hailar, which was invaded by a large number of soldiers on R and R as various regiments took turns having a day off throughout the week.

That evening we entered the gate of the One Hundred Eighteenth Regiment of the Kwantung Army. Sixteen of us were placed in one squad, and each of us in turn was interviewed by the personnel officer, and I was the last one. From my records, the officer knew I was born in the United States. He gave me a stern warning that I was to work extra hard to prove my loyalty to Japan because of my birthplace. He mentioned that my parents in America had been sent to a concentration camp and told me how important it was for me to become a good Japanese soldier and fight and even die, if necessary, for Japan.

Now I would be fighting with weapon in hand against the country of my birth. I was relieved that I was stationed in Manchuria, not in the South Pacific, where I would actually be in battle against American soldiers, perhaps even my own brother among them. I accepted my fate to fight for Japan as an "adopted" Japanese, but at the same time I did not have a strong sense that Americans were my enemy. As strange and confused as it may sound, the Doolittle raid on Tokyo or the sight of B-29 formations flying overhead on their bombing runs did not evoke in me an enormous amount of hostility or hatred toward Americans.

I recalled the time in Tokyo when one of my classmates at school and I saw a formation of warplanes flying above us. My friend said, "Look at those planes; we've got a lot of them, and we are strong enough to defeat Americans. See, we are well prepared for a war with the country you came from. How about that?" It was clear that he looked on me as his enemy. There were other such occasions when my schoolmates would talk to me as if I were not a Japanese like them but an American. They would compare the two countries and say that Japan was superior, implying that they and theirs were better than I and whatever I represented. I looked back on my days in America, where sometimes I was not treated as a true American, and now, here in Japan, I realized that I was not considered a true Japanese either. It was as though I did not really belong to either country.

By the time I went into my squad room, everyone had turned in. I sat in utter darkness. My heart was heavy. Here I was, about to begin group living, which I never liked; worse, this group living was that of the military. Sadness, anger, and despair over this turn of events was more than I could bear. I felt as if I had been thrown into a dark, cold, and bottomless pit from which there was no escape.

5. First Lesson as an Orderly: Mopping Is Easier with Hot Water

I was one of sixteen recruits assigned to Squad 4, Company Headquarters, Second Battalion, 118th Regiment of the Kwantung Army. Our squad occupied the top floor of a two-story building. The building was built of bricks and was well insulated, with double-paned sash windows to protect its occupants from the harsh winter of northern Manchuria. I later learned that the 118th Regiment buildings were quite new and among the best in the entire Kwantung Army. Each squad room housed two rows of bunks on two levels divided by a center corridor where two long tables and benches were placed on both sides for us to use for eating meals and writing. The upper bunks were usually occupied by the senior soldiers, while we, the new recruits, were given the lower bunks. At the end of each bunk, against the wall, was an unpainted wooden box for small personal effects, and a set of clean clothes was placed next to the box, folded and in a neat stack.

Sergeants Kariya and Homma of the squad had a private room by the stairway to our floor and had two soldiers assigned to them as orderlies, who cleaned the room, served meals, polished their boots, did their laundry, and even were expected to wash their backs when the squad went to bathe. Generally, being an orderly was considered a lot of extra work, but all privates were to take their turn at this assignment sometime during their basic training. It was my good fortune to be paired up for this duty

with PFC Imai, with whom I had shared the small mattress in Hakata. Imai had two older brothers in the military who had passed on to him the vital shortcuts necessary for accomplishing this duty successfully.

Imai was a tall and handsome man with long, dark eyebrows. A college student at the time he was recruited, he was a smooth operator who knew all the shortcuts and the easiest ways to do tasks in the least amount of time possible. He was quite entertaining and popular among the soldiers and superiors alike. Because his two older brothers were serving in the military in the South Pacific and his parents had given up hope of seeing them back home alive, he was the one who was expected to take over the responsibilities of the family eventually. He, therefore, turned down all suggestions made by his superiors that he participate in an officers' training program.

Every morning after roll call, Imai and I, as orderlies, ran toward the sergeants' room, stopped outside the door to knock, and entered when a voice from within answered, "Enter." The two of us would step in, line up side by side, and shout at the top of our voices, "PFC Imai has come to clean up the sergeants' room! PFC Suzuki has come to clean up the sergeants' room!" During the first week or so, I often forgot to knock or unintentionally left out the shouting. Whoever was in the room turned around and looked up with a nasty glitter in his eyes as if to say,

"Ha, ha, gotcha that time," and barked, "Go back out, and do it over!" It seemed that the army was a place where soldiers were not allowed to make mistakes; if they did, their superiors got pleasure out of it, and of making them do it over correctly, or sometimes rewarding them with a sock in the face.

Cleaning the sergeants' room meant making the bunks, sweeping, and mopping the floor with cold water. Mopping, however, was much easier with hot water. For Imai, it was not too difficult to arrange this by sneaking off with a bucket of hot water from the boiler early in the morning when no one was around. One morning, he told me I should go get the hot water. He went through all the dos and don'ts to avoid getting caught by the much-dreaded third-year soldier who was a perpetual private and in charge of the hot water tank.

I left on this "mission" with much trepidation. Everything was going well until I turned around to leave with the bucket filled with hot water. I felt a tap on my back. "What's all that hot water for? Don't tell me your squad's already through eating this morning and this is for washing the utensils. I ain't even seen any group come to get their rice and soup yet," the voice from behind said, sounding unmistakably pleased to catch a new recruit in a wrong act. "Gotta think fast. Gotta think fast." My heart was pounding. Putting the bucket down, I turned around and found myself face to face with the infamous soldier with the small razor scar on his lower left cheek. The hot water was primarily for washing dishes after a meal, and I remembered my buddies' warning against being caught by this soldier for even a "second helping" of hot water during the course of one meal. "If he saw you do that," they said, "he would take the empty bucket from you, and put it over your head, and beat on it with a large wooden ladle until he knocked you over."

"Yes, no, senior-year soldier. I, PFC Suzuki, have come to get hot water to wash the company commander's plates that were left unwashed from last night," I said with a straight face. I had my fingers crossed, hoping he wouldn't notice that the bucket was marked MOPPING, not FOR WASHING DISHES. There was a long, tense pause. "OK! Don't you guys know that you ain't supposed to leave dirty dishes overnight? I'll let you go this time; take it and go." "Yes, Sir. Many thanks for your trouble." I did not forget to add the "Many thanks for your trouble," for I had learned that in the army it was like a period in a sentence. We were expected to repeat this "chant" throughout the day on various occasions. I picked up the bucket and hurried back to the sergeants' room, where I found Imai waiting for me.

"What's wrong, Suzuki? You're white as a ghost," Imai whispered, as we were washing our mops in the bucket. I envied Imai for being so calm, always composed and observant, noticing the slightest move or change even when there were superiors around and work to be done. "I'll tell you later," I whispered back. Imai was not satisfied with that for an answer. He was insistent. "Didn't get caught, did you? Gotta watch out. We can't do this mopping with cold water, you know." "Yeah, that scar-face PFC got me. But I told him this was for washing the company commander's plates from last night." Imai looked at me with an approving smile, as if to say, "You're catching on." He often told me that "using good judgment" was an old and favorite expression in the army. It was simply a basic survival method for a soldier to try to make everything he does look good in the eyes of his superiors while, at the same time, making work as easy as possible for himself.

Every morning after completing our chores at the sergeants' room, Imai and I would return to our own squad room to find our breakfast waiting for us. If we finished our job too soon and Imai thought that it would be too early to go back to our room, he would dust the shelves for the second time, unfold the sergeants' shirts and refold them, straighten out the shoes more than once, and do those things deliberately and slowly. He was using his "good judgment" to see that the timing was just right, and we were greeted with a burst of "Many thanks for your trouble" from our buddies when we returned to the squad room.

One morning I mentioned to Imai that maybe we should get back to our room after finishing the sergeants' room and help set up the table and do the other routine chores rather than dragging out our work. Imai brushed off the suggestion and said, "Heck, it's all right to let those other guys think we're having a hard time with our duties. They'll all get their turn at it, and if they find it easy, they'll feel just like I do. If they don't, it's their tough luck 'cause they don't have good judgment. Don't let it bother you, Suzuki."

We were allowed to do the laundry only on the day our squad was the last group to bathe, which was every three or four days, since we were to use the bathwater for the laundry. As an orderly, I had a double load of laundry to do, the sergeants' and my own, within a limited amount of time. To save time, I avoided sleeping between the sheets, sleeping instead sandwiched between the blankets so that I did not need to do my own sheets.

We also took care of the sergeants' meals, delivering each meal to their room and going back to clear the table after finishing our own meal. The sergeants were always considerate enough to leave a small portion of food on the plates for us. They acted as though they couldn't finish it, but, of course, we knew the leftovers were intended for the hungry recruits.

Food was far from abundant. Although we were not starving, any extra was most welcome. One night, when the lieutenant was out of town, his orderly got into the kitchen and stole some rice, which he made into rice balls and hid under a wash pan in the lieutenant's room. The soldier woke me up in the middle of the night, and, pretending that we were headed for the latrine, we sneaked into the lieutenant's room and devoured the rice balls in the dark. As the soldier reported to the room early the next morning, he found grains of rice on the floor tracing our steps of the night before. Luckily, however, they were not noticed by the lieutenant.

When the weather was warmer, we went out to pick some weed called *akaza*, a plant similar to the dandelion, which we "cooked" as a supplement to our dinner by putting it in the wire basket with our dishes, which were boiled after each meal to sanitize them. Whenever it was our turn to set the table and serve the meal, we packed our own rice bowls and our buddies' with as much rice as we could put into them. We could not deny our preoccupation with food. Signs of hunger were all around us.

6. Learning to Fight without Weapons

Although the 118th was a heavy artillery regiment, the company to which I belonged was Company Headquarters, and our training was limited to functions that would support a command post. Soon the sixteen recruits broke up into four different groups, to train in wireless communication, telephone communication, reconnaissance, and transportation. I was placed in the telephone communication group, again with Imai.

It was almost May, and each day felt warmer than the day before. In Manchuria, or at least in the region where we were stationed, the snow was not deep, yet the ground was frozen much of the time, covered with a thin layer of snow even in late April. One day I found a blade of green grass breaking through the ground, and, before we knew it, we found ourselves surrounded by a carpet of tiny purple flowers. The Manchurians called the flower *en chu pha*, "a flower that knows the spring." Leaves were budding on the trees, and the entire countryside seemed to be turning green. Indeed, spring had come. As if to respond to the flowers and the warm sunshine, the soldiers seemed more human, lighthearted, and pleasant to each other. We would take lunch and go out for training, leaving the barracks behind.

Sergeant Seki, training instructor for the group, acted as if he were treating us to a family outing. We were divided into two groups, each group taking a position on the opposite side of a rolling green hill, about half a mile away from each other, in order to practice using the telephone. Hailar, home for a number of regiments of the Kwantung Army, had rolling hills and a higher hill on which a fortress had been built. The fortress stretched for many miles. The military described it as being as well equipped as the Maginot Line or the Siegfried Line in Europe. By the time we arrived there, however, it had been completely stripped of weapons. We were told much later that the Russians who went into the fortress after Japan's surrender found nothing stored in it but stale *yokan*, a kind of Japanese cake made of red beans.

Sergeant Seki was born and raised in Tokyo and had never lived anywhere else until he was sent to Manchuria. Imai soon found out about this, and whenever Sergeant Seki ordered a short break during our training, he would go over to join Seki and begin talking about Tokyo; how the B-29s were bombing Tokyo, what sections were hit, and just about anything he could think of that might hold Seki's interest and keep him from ordering us back to drilling again. Imai was doing an excellent job of it, too, for every time a short break was called, supposedly only time enough to smoke one cigarette, it lasted for twenty to thirty minutes and sometimes even an hour when the other recruits pitched in to do their share in occupying Seki with stories about Tokyo.

I look back on those days with amazement, a few months before Japan's surrender in August 1945. It makes one wonder why on earth people in Japan did not raise questions about the very clear signs that Japan's war efforts were fast coming to an end, without weapons or any military supplies with which to continue fighting. On the home front, students of high school age, who had been recruited to work in weapons factories on school days, found themselves simply pretending to work and looking busy when the factory supervisor came around to inspect them. They no longer had any raw material to work with. Although they were allowed to return to school one day a week to "study," part of that day was spent in training in the use of bamboo spears, the only weapons with which to confront enemy soldiers in case they landed on Japanese soil!

Hailar also showed sad signs of the desperate situation. Most of the garages at the 118th Regiment stood empty. This regiment had a reputation as one of the most mechanized heavy artillery units in the Japanese Army, but now most of their weapons had been sent to the South Pacific. The transportation unit of our regiment had no supply of gasoline, and, as a result, its training consisted of a soldier sitting in the driver's seat of the truck and going through the motions of driving while the rest of the soldiers got behind the vehicle to push it. I do not know what went through the minds of those soldiers as they were going through these ridiculous motions and calling it "training." I wondered what they thought they would or could do had there been an enemy attack. I was reminded of the slogan, "A drop of fuel is equal to a drop of blood," which so accurately described the situation in Japan then. In contrast, I thought of my father's farm in Imperial Valley, where, on cold winter mornings, the tractor drivers would pour gasoline into a five-gallon can, which they would light and use as a stove to warm themselves.

Saturday evenings were the times for our talent shows, which provided minimal entertainment. Everyone was expected to take part by doing something. I hated these gatherings; I felt that I had no talent to share and was extremely uncomfortable about performing in front of people. Having no choice in the matter, however, I decided to sing a well-known Japanese song, "Yashi no mi," a song about a lonely traveler lamenting his rootless life miles away from home. I translated the Japanese words into English as I sang but told the audience that I was singing in Malaysian. English, "the language of the enemy," was, of course, unacceptable in those days. Imai was the only one who knew what I was doing and gave me a knowing look. I was sure, however, that there were others who were aware of my background and therefore my faking. I finished my act, took a bow, and sat down. After the customary applause, nothing else was said. Imai, on the other hand, was a ham. Whatever act he performed was highly entertaining and appreciated by all, but he confided to me that, in spite of his success, he did not enjoy performing for the group as much as his audience enjoyed him. He was, nevertheless, a talented man.

The soldiers sang a great deal, mostly patriotic songs, in the evenings after their work was done for the day. I only mouthed words along with them, as I did not know the songs that they knew by heart. We also did sumo (Japanese wrestling). I remembered how strong I was when I was in school and could beat most of the classmates who would challenge me. But now I was weak and no longer able to win many of the matches. Life in the army, with much regimentation and no personal freedom or privacy, was beginning to take its toll. I was no longer the person I had been.

7. Death of a Soldier

The shortage in manpower in Japan must have been critical during the last six months of the war, although that fact was never made public or admitted by the Japanese government. We had in our squad a recruit who was almost illiterate and another who looked extremely pale and coughed incessantly. Each of us was given a chart that was to be kept daily as a way for our superiors to know how we were adjusting to life in the army. We were required to fill in the number of times we coughed, how often nature called, whether we went to sleep before we heard taps, whether we slept until reveille, and other such items. For me, neither reveille nor taps was necessary, because the stress of strictly regimented army life kept me wide awake even after taps and woke me before the bugle sounded. The sergeants checked the chart every day to see how each of us was doing in general, while the medic paid particular attention to physical aspects of adjustment.

PFC Saito's figures in the column under the heading coughing were steadily increasing; as a result, he was ordered to visit the regiment dispensary for a checkup. When we returned from our training one evening, we found Saito lying down in his bunk wearing a large white gauze mask that covered his mouth and nose. Looking about, and making sure that there were no superiors within hearing distance, we took turns approaching Saito's bunk and whispered, "You lucky guy, you! You stay here and have it easy, while we go out and have to sweat like hell." Saito answered weakly, "What do you mean, 'lucky'? Can't you see I'm coughing?" Although he would not admit it, he, too, felt that he was better off than his buddies. He was as yet unaware that he was tubercular and that his condition had already reached an advanced stage. The soldier who slept next to Saito proceeded to do Saito's share of the chores after he finished his own.

As the days went by, Saito grew weaker and now was running a fever. There was no doubt, after a week, that he had to be sent to the army hospital. The recruits still spoke of his "good fortune" as they compared his hospitalization to the daily grind of training that they were going through.

Two weeks later the squad sergeants took Imai and me with them to the hospital to visit Saito. Patients were moving slowly, shuffling in their slippers down the hospital corridor. They were in white robes in the kimono style, the same robes I saw in Tokyo on the wounded soldiers who had been sent back from the battlefield. Doctors and their aides whisked by as we walked toward a big room where Saito lay. He looked ashen. He knew he would never see his homeland again. "I don't think I'll last much longer," said Saito in a barely audible voice. "You know, I admit now that I thought I had it made, not having to run around like you guys, but I feel different now. I'll tell you, watch your health, and tell my other buddies that, too. To die in a hospital bed is not giving one's life to the emperor and the country. I regret that, but anyhow, thanks for coming, and do thank the guys for all they've done for me, will you?"

It was only three days later that the squad was notified of Saito's death and his posthumous promotion to corporal. The sergeants, Imai and I, and two other recruits went in a truck to take Saito for his last ride. We drove to the far edge of town. The orange sky of the sunset was in brilliant contrast to the dark-hued flatland that stretched for miles and miles. The coffin, which was a plain wooden box, was taken off the truck and placed on a pile of firewood. We poured gasoline on it and lit a match. The crim-

son flames burst and leapt toward the sky with energy and fury that Saito had surely not known during his brief life in the army. The smoke was thick and black, and the coffin rocked slightly as the firewood underneath began to crumble. As the sky gradually darkened, the flames of the fire died down. Sergeant Kariya, visibly shaken by the death of one of his men, muttered, "What a way to go! You've got to watch your health, all of you."

I looked at my fellow soldiers standing around the embers and felt a sudden closeness to all as this superior, not at all conscious of his rank or ours, shared his deep sense of loss, grief, and caring for all his men. Sergeant Kariya also knew that he was the one who had the difficult job of writing to Saito's family to inform them of his untimely death. I said to myself, "Poor guy, I wouldn't want to go like this." I had no way of knowing then what was in store for me and how often I would reflect on this episode with a feeling akin to envy.

It was dark by the time we returned to our barracks. We got off the truck and walked in silence toward the entrance door. I could hear only the sound of our boots on the concrete walkway.

Sadness still lingered as we took off our boots, put on our slippers, and went up the stairs to our room.

The rest of the squad were going about their routine, the older soldiers sitting together and chatting, the recruits busy with their chores. Our meal was waiting for us in one corner of the table. The rice, the *miso* soup, and the cooked vegetables had grown cold. As Imai and I sat down to eat, a couple of the soldiers came over and asked in a whisper about the afternoon. The rest only looked toward us now and then and did not come speak to us. Yet I somehow knew that all of us were acutely aware of Saito's absence and shared a sense that we had grown in a way that can come only from being in a situation where death is a real part of life.

8. Surrender: The Beginning Rather Than the End

Even for me, army life had fallen into a predictable pattern. Amid the flurry of activities, my four months of basic training at Hailar went by swiftly. In early July, those of us who had completed high school and beyond were interviewed and urged to apply for officers' training. We were given a written examination, which, it became obvious, was little more than a formality; it appeared that all who took the test were accepted into the program. I was among the hundred who gathered in front of the regimental headquarters building a few weeks later to be shipped to training camp in the Great Khingan Mountain Range, which was the divide between northern and southern Manchuria.

Concurrently with our departure, not only our entire regiment but also most of the soldiers in the entire military town of Hailar were transferred to various parts of the same mountain range to engage in so-called fortification projects. Hence, what remained at the 118th Regiment was only a small skeleton force of fewer than one hundred men. Before all this movement began, Imai had confided in me that he had heard the company commander tell our sergeants that there were mysterious lights seen around the periphery of the regimental compound. No one knew exactly what those lights were, but a few guessed that they might be enemy agents scouting the setup of the regiment. Was this the reason that our training was to take place in the remote area of the mountains and the reason that the entire regiment was moved? It was an ominous sign of the tragic and frightful events that were to befall us shortly.

My benefactor Imai was one of the soldiers who stayed behind at Hailar. Determined to stay out of officers' training, he did not disclose that he was qualified to apply, mainly because of his parents' strong objection to his "volunteering" to become an officer. I was never to see or hear from him again. We had experienced many things together during our brief basic training, and thanks to his ability and shared knowledge, army life was much more bearable for me. Hailar was overrun by the Red Army immediately after the Soviet Union entered the war against Japan for the last ten days of World War II. I shudder and feel deep sorrow at the thought that perhaps he was killed in the brief skirmish with the invading Soviet soldiers. But then, knowing his great sense of timing, I want to believe that he survived and eventually returned safely to his parents in Japan.

Officers' training was grueling mentally as well as physically. As soon as we arrived, we were issued rifles, and our training began, concentrating on exercises designed for the infantry branch of the army. There were forced marches almost daily, and on one occasion we left camp at seven in the evening and marched all night, returning at noon the next day without any rest except for short, ten- to fifteen-minute breaks. We did not have a bite to eat either. A few fell by the wayside; I do not know how I survived. I reached camp with blistered feet and aching muscles, completely exhausted, to say the least.

Only a week into this exercise, we were completely surprised and bewildered when our instructing officer gathered us together and announced, "I have just received orders from my superior to cancel this program immediately. All of you are to return to your own company. Do not forget what you have learned here during this brief time. Also, do not forget that you are to become leaders. Therefore, when you return to your company, be proud, and always be an example for others to follow. I am positive that we will resume our training again soon. Until then, take care, and be good soldiers."

We returned to our old company for the so-called fortification projects. I found out later that this was when the Soviet government entered the war against Japan. Back with the company, I found the soldiers busy digging caves into the mountain. At the first opportunity, I approached one of my buddies and asked, "What are we digging these caves for? Are they shelters to get ready for winter?" "Of course not. Haven't you been told? They're for our big guns, artillery. We're going to place them in here. The entire regiment from Hailar is up here in the mountains, and there are caves like this being dug all over, and, I guess, some are shelters, too." "Where are the artillery coming from?" I persisted with my questions. "Back from Hailar, I guess," he answered, although he did not sound too certain of anything he was saying.

Some dynamite was used to help blast the large boulders. However, most of the digging and removing of rocks was primitive: soldiers with a hammer or a chisel in hand pounded away at the massive wall of rock. I thought of sculptors as I stood there watching this scene. It could have been humorous if it were not so pathetic. Just as primitive was the way in which the chipped stone was carried away, with two soldiers carrying on their shoulders a pole from which hung a crude basket filled with chunks of rock. The hot summer sun blazed down from the clear blue sky as we toiled away, not questioning what we were ordered to do, and sometimes even pausing and congratulating each other when someone succeeded in breaking off a piece of boulder too large to be hauled away in a single basket.

While at this task, I thought of my kendo (Japanese fencing) instructor in Tokyo, a retired navy captain, who had been called back to active duty and was serving in the South Pacific theater. He visited the school on one of his leaves to give a talk to the student body. In his talk, he reported that the enemy had constructed an airfield overnight by laying down sheets of metal. He also said that the enemy tanks sounded as smooth as an aircraft in the sky, in contrast to the rumbling Japanese tanks, suggesting that they were far superior weapons mechanically. He must have seriously doubted if Japan could ever win the war in the Pacific.

The accommodations in the mountain cave were simple. They were constructed mostly with birch trees, which grew in great abundance at this high altitude. Hundreds of birch trees were left standing, but stripped of their bark, which had been used to thatch the roof of our shelter. Although their roundish gray-green leaves shimmered in the sunshine of the brief northern summer, the trees stood there like countless victims whose clothing was stolen and were left naked, to die in a short time.

It was several days after returning and rejoining my company that I heard in the far distance the rumble of heavy artillery echoing through the mountains and canyons. That evening, down in the valley far below us, we spotted a tiny, dark object. Looking through his binoculars, the company commander said, "It's a Soviet tank! I think it's out on a reconnaissance mission." "Man, they're sure foolhardy! It's as if they're challenging us to shoot," said the sergeant as he took the binoculars to look.

Our regular supper became a little party that night. There was an air of forced festivity, bristling with tension. What most of us had in mind was that this would be our last supper before going into battle the next day. Beer was brought out and served. It was my first taste of this beverage, and as I drank it and felt the fizzy liquid go down, I thought to myself, "Wow! How good this is! What have I been missing all this time?" One of the senior soldiers who had just returned from a liaison mission to the town showed up with a chicken he had stolen from a farm on his way back. Visibly proud and pleased with his booty, he rolled up his sleeves to prepare a fancy meal of raw meat. (In Japan, when prepared properly by an experienced chef, raw chicken breast is considered a delicacy.) The senior soldiers did not share the chicken with those of us who were mere recruits; it turned out to be our good fortune, for those who ate it became very ill that evening. They received little sympathy from us as their vomiting and diarrhea continued into the night.

It was midnight when we were awakened by the night guard, who came into our tent and yelled that everyone was to get up and prepare to leave within twenty minutes. The night air in the high mountains was cold; I could not keep my teeth from chattering. Somehow, I felt that it was not only the chill of the night but something else that was causing me to tremble. "Something must be wrong. Here we are, leaving our tents and most of our belongings behind, not knowing where we are headed or if we will ever return," I thought. I left behind that night the *hara-maki* that my mother had made for me and in it the one-hundred-yen bill that she had pressed into my hand that morning for me to keep for some unforeseen emergency. I grabbed my rifle, strapped on my bayonet, and swung my small pack across my back. Along with all the others, I stood in the small clearing in front of the tents. The stars glimmered in the dark sky. The company commander was standing in front of us and barked out the order that we begin our march.

We trudged down the mountain the rest of the night and arrived at a small town at early dawn. We went to the train station, where we sat on the ground to await further orders. The train station looked somewhat like the one back home. I lay on my back and gazed at the surrounding mountains as the sun came up. I must have fallen asleep, for when I woke up, the voices I heard were not those of the folks at home sending me off but the talking, shouting, and crying of men, women, and children, all Japanese civilians, on a freight train that had just pulled into the station. I soon learned that they had evacuated their homes in the northern part of Manchuria and were heading south.

The open freight cars were crowded with refugees; it was even more crowded when the soldiers climbed aboard. I scrambled aboard a car that seemed least crowded. I detected a tinge of disbelief, fear, and confusion in the eyes of the people, who had evidently lost the security of home and livelihood so suddenly. The train soon pulled out of the station and chugged on. It stopped at each small station along the way as even more people climbed aboard. Looking about me in the open car, I recalled scenes that I had seen when I was a child in America from the "Fox Movie-Tone News" of the civil war in Spain. I was now thrown in the midst of the same kind of confusion and chaos.

The day wore on; toward evening, when the train stopped again, I got off to buy something to eat from the Manchurian farmers who were gathered around the train selling vegetables and other food. There I overheard a young Japanese man, dressed in civilian clothes but carrying a rifle, telling one of the soldiers that the emperor himself was on the radio to let his people know that Japan had surrendered. "Impossible," I thought, and quickly tried to put it out of my mind. After all, we were still carrying our rifles, and, besides, we believed that the Japanese would fight to the very last rather than face the humiliation of surrender. As soon as I got back on the train, I repeated what I just heard to a soldier sitting next to me. "What, Japan surrender?" he exclaimed, with disgust and anger in his voice. "Impossible! How dare you say such a thing! We're retreating to some place in central Manchuria to regroup for an offensive!"

The train continued its journey south and came to the small town of Flargi, situated about fifteen miles south of Chichihaerh, a large city in central Manchuria. We were ordered to get off the train at this small town and proceeded to an army camp that had once served as a convalescent center for soldiers who had suffered long hospitalizations. It was after 10:00 P.M. when we arrived at our destination, exhausted. The barracks had been evacuated and had been stripped bare of furnishings. Lying down on the floor, I went over in my mind all that had happened since the middle of the night when we were awakened and ordered to descend the mountain. I thought about those frantic refugees with whom we shared the train ride.

As day broke, we found out how badly vandalized this place

was. One of the rooms was strewn with papers marked CLASSI-
FIED and TOP SECRET as well as some Japanese paper money and
coins. The vegetable field was also picked almost clean. We found
some melons about the size of a baseball still left in the field,
which we picked and ate with relish. There was no clean water,
but we found a storeroom with cases of sake.

Later that day, we were ordered to muster and take our rifles
to another army installation not too far from the convalescent
center. To our astonishment, we were ordered to turn in our
rifles and bayonets there, the only weapons we had with us at
that time. There was already a pile of rifles on the ground in the
yard. I walked up to this pile and threw my rifle on the heap. I
unbuckled my belt and did the same with the bayonet. For a
brief few moments, I felt as if parts of my body were being ripped
off. The harsh sound of metal hitting metal pierced my ears.
Every rifle in the Japanese Army carried the imperial crest on it
and was considered sacred and as such was to be protected from
any mishandling. Between the soldier's life and the rifle's safe-

keeping, it was the rifle that had priority. This idea, so emphasized in military training even from school days, was deeply ingrained in every soldier. But now, we were tossing our rifles into a careless heap. Those in command continued to refer to this as "returning" weapons, never "surrendering" them, as they were not willing to accept the reality that Japan had lost the war.

Without my rifle or bayonet, I felt naked as we marched back to the first camp. The sight and sound of the heap of weapons were still fresh in my mind. That evening we were ordered to depart for Chichihaerh, taking with us only our rucksack and a canteen, which we filled with sake sweetened with sugar. Not having our weapons made our load that much lighter and reinforced our feeling that we were leaving something important behind. Whenever we stopped for a short break, some men lay flat on their backs along the dirt road, which was a levee higher than the surrounding fields, to catch whatever rest they could. Others went off the road to urinate, as the sake took effect.

At one of those stops, I heard some commotion. It was dusk. I walked up the road twenty or thirty yards to see what it was all about. My eyes caught a sight that sent a chill down my spine. There was an old man, a bearded Manchurian peasant, lying face up, arms and legs spread out, slashed across the torso from neck to waist with a samurai sword. His clothes and the ground around him were covered with blood, which was now dry and discolored. Someone speculated that perhaps he was caught stealing or the victim of robbery himself.

As we resumed our walk, we spotted a bright fire ahead. We found a burning horse cart loaded with what looked like household goods. The slain man and the burning cart, on top of all the other things we had witnessed in the last two days, were a sign that there were drastic changes afoot; whether we realized it or not, we too were part of the confusion and tragedy of a lost war.

We continued marching along the road, which was now wider and surfaced with gravel. An order was relayed from the rear of the column to move over to one side of the road. It was daybreak, and for the first time we saw Soviet soldiers, who were riding on large amphibious landing craft. They smiled and waved at us as they passed by. They were followed by more soldiers in huge ten-wheeled Studebaker trucks bearing U.S. Army numbers on the hoods. There were more vehicles after them, loaded with broken chairs, tables, and sundry other goods. "Thieves at a fire!" sneered some of the Japanese soldiers. We were to learn later that the invading Soviet soldiers took everything they could lay their hands on and transported it back to Siberia. We marched on until midday and finally came to the city of Chichihaerh. The bewildered civilians walking the streets, I thought, were much like those I had seen in Tokyo when I entered the army six months earlier.

We came on a large gate shaded by tall trees growing on both sides. The column stopped in front of the gate. Many of the people on the street stopped to look at us. Some of us sat down on the ground but were promptly ordered to stand up. Even though we were in the shade, it was very warm. I looked up into the trees. There was no breeze at all, and the leaves were still. "I wonder what we're going to do in there," I heard a voice behind me say. Just then, the gates were pushed open from the inside by two Soviet soldiers. They were not smiling like those we saw earlier that morning riding in the convoys. An order was given, and we stood at attention. "Forward march!" came the next command. Strictly in military fashion, we marched through the gate in perfect pace and entered the base.

The gates closed, and our life as prisoners of the Russians began.

9. Learning the Tricks of Prison Camp

We spent our first week in prison camp doing odd jobs within the confines of the tall wooden wall with the barbed wire on top. We pulled weeds around the barracks and cleared the area around the fence of weeds and brush. Rumor had it that the Russians feared the prisoners might hide behind the grown brush, sneak up to the wall, and climb over it to escape. On the long train ride to Krasnoyarsk, I remembered seeing an armed guard at each end of the many bridges we crossed. We learned that we were five to six hundred miles from Mongolia; the thought of escape was not entirely out of the realm of possibility. It was, however, little more than a far-off dream for us with such barriers to discourage any attempt.

Other odd jobs involved cleaning the windows and piling the earth for the berm against the barracks wall. As we went about doing those simple, menial jobs, we wondered if we had been brought all this long distance to do such trivial tasks. "Don't be foolish," warned an older prisoner as he overheard our conversation. "The Russians will have us do all sorts of labor soon. I tell you we'll probably be here till next spring working in that factory we saw when we got off the train." He was right—only he was completely off the mark as far as the duration of our stay was concerned.

In our second week at the camp, we were put into work groups of ten to fifty for various tasks inside and around the factory. We were engaged in such work as digging trenches for pipes, loading and unloading freight trains, and general cleanup around the huge factory. Of the two thousand imprisoned in Krasnoyarsk Camp 5, only a handful remained within the wall, assigned to jobs related directly to the operation of the camp, such as personnel work at the headquarters office, kitchen, and dispensary.

At seven o'clock each morning, the long steel bar hanging outside the camp headquarters clanged with an ugly echo, the most dreaded sound, and one we wished we could do without, as if this merciless signal in the morning were totally responsible for the hard and dreary daily routine that followed. The prisoners staggered out of the barracks and lined up inside the walls in front of the gate to be counted before they were taken to their work stations in the factory by the guards.

Some of the guards apparently had little education compared to the prisoners they were guarding. I heard insulting rumors that Russian soldiers would wear two and three wristwatches on each arm without knowing they needed to be wound. They acquired the watches, we were told, by trading tobacco with the prisoners; some were even confiscated. I paid little attention to these exaggerated stories until one day I found that the guard who took us to work was unable to count the number of men in his group. Each time we left the camp, two Russian officers were at the gate to count us. The guard then signed his name to the book and was responsible for returning the exact same number of prisoners at the end of the day. When we gathered at the job site at the end of the shift, it was the guard's responsibility to make sure that all the men in his charge were there. He needed to rely on one of the prisoners to help him verify that he had the right number of prisoners.

Many months later, when a Russian officer came to the headquarters to inquire how many among us could read, he refused to believe the reply that every prisoner was literate. The Russians were making plans at that time to print a newspaper in Japanese and needed to know how many copies to distribute to our camp. This newspaper was published weekly primarily for the purpose of disseminating anti-American propaganda and carrying articles against the Marshall Plan and stories critical of the operations of the American Occupation Forces in Japan.

Some Russians who were our job foremen also showed their lack of basic math knowledge when they simply did not accept the way we came up with the total number of bricks on a flatbed railcar by multiplying the number of bricks in length, width, and height. The Russian civilian workers also asked the prisoners questions about a wide variety of things, assuming that we would have answers to everything. If a prisoner did not know the answer to their question, they became annoyed and angry, thinking that the Japanese knew but was withholding the information. In spite of the fact that some guards were unable to count, that the officers did not accept that all prisoners were able to read a newspaper, and that they were suspicious that we were withholding information from them, the relationship between the Russians and the prisoners was generally quite amicable.

The Russians in general, it seemed to us, did not have a great deal of animosity toward the Japanese, perhaps because the two nations were not engaged in this war for very long and, therefore, the sense that the Japanese had been their enemies was not strong. On the other hand, we were told, they were bitter toward Germany, which had caused much suffering in Russia at the time of its invasion, and, consequently, the German prisoners sent to Siberia were treated much more harshly than we were. Looking back on those days, many of us could have benefited more from our experience there if we had attempted to learn their language and gain more knowledge about the country and people. But we were simply too tired, too hungry, and devoid of hope for the future.

As the days grew shorter, the thermometer began to register subfreezing temperatures. It became harder and harder to dig trenches as the ground was frozen solid. The Russians seemed not to give much thought to the work quota they set for each of us. If the quota for one man was to dig a cubic yard of earth, it was the same whether it was soft sand, gravel, or earth frozen as hard as rock. To make matters worse, even the tools given to us worked against us. Most of the shovels were poorly manufactured, without a sharp edge for digging, and were heavy and awkward to handle. Trying to remedy the problems, we complained frequently to the Russians, but to no avail. We had no choice but to continue our work under these difficult conditions.

The prisoners, however, were catching on, learning the tricks that allowed them to cope with the situation. I first experienced this when I was sent out with a group to load a flat railcar with coal that had been unloaded earlier at a spot away from the plant. Now we were ordered to move it to the factory. The group was divided into two, with some of the men working on top of the car, the rest remaining on the ground below. We were working with our overweight shovels. As we threw the coal onto the flatbed of the railcar, the men on top moved and piled the coal in such a way that there was a high mound around the perimeter of the bed. It was like a loaf of bread that failed to rise in the oven, its middle caved in. The car then had the appearance of carrying a full load when viewed from the ground. We moved on to our next task. As soon as we came up with this trick, the Russian foreman on our next load pointed at the car spring and argued that it did not indicate the tension that it should if the load were full. A brief argument ensued, which we won. As we moved on to our next task, our Japanese leader said, "I knew we wouldn't have to argue too hard. Our foreman gets credit for the amount of work we do—so if we can make a good showing, it's that much credit for him." We used this method to make our work easier when loading other materials on a flatbed car, too.

There were times when work was slow. We knew that the Russian foreman would call his office and come up with some extra work if he found us standing around empty-handed. To avoid this, two or even three of us got together to do work that really required only one person to handle. Sometimes it was obvious that we were shirking our work, and the foreman tried his best to break us up. We then pretended that we didn't understand what he was saying and did our best to appear to be struggling to do our task. We usually got our way, although not always.

Among the various odd jobs to which we were assigned during the early period, unloading coal cars was the most dreaded. When a long coal train pulled onto a spur track, the Japanese leader of the group, together with the Russian foreman, divided the group into smaller teams of three or four men, depending on the number of cars and the number of men in the group. When the temperature dropped far below freezing, the coal often came frozen inside the railcars, making it extremely difficult for us to unload. The general rule for unloading coal cars was that if a team was lucky enough to be assigned to an "easy load" and completed its unloading early, that team was allowed to go to a warm shed or some enclosure to wait there until the entire group completed their jobs. However, sometimes they were called back to assist a team working on a "bad load."

I encountered both "easy" and "bad" loads. It was a freezing cold night in early November when our team hit a bad load. To begin with, we got a very late start, having great difficulty getting the sliding doors open on our car. (Usually, the coal came in regular boxcars.) The hangers for the sliding doors were broken, and they would not budge. After struggling with them for what seemed a very long time, we finally managed to get them open and climbed in. We noticed that those in the next car were already halfway through their load. On the spot, we decided that we were not going to empty our car completely. Less than halfway through our load, we saw that the teams on the next two cars had already completed their unloading and were walking toward the shed. We also saw our Russian foreman walk past our car toward the other end of the train. We all jumped off the car at that moment and, after much struggle, finally got the doors closed. We felt safe, as we knew that the foreman could not open the door himself to see if the car had been completely unloaded. Feigning to have done a very efficient job, we dashed into the shed.

Once, when I was on a night shift, a long train of cars came into the coal yard. There were not enough men to make teams of an adequate size. Only two men were allotted for an eighteen-ton car and four men for a forty-ton car. I was placed on a four-man team. We stood along the tracks as the train slowly backed into the yard. It was still moving when all the teams dashed out and climbed aboard the boxcars and began opening the doors. Some of the more efficient teams were already shoveling off the coal from the moving cars. Our team, too, stood inside the car and began pushing the coal out the door. "Hey, we're lucky!" I shouted, "The coal is pretty dry, and it's not frozen underneath." "Let's poke the holes," my teammate chimed in. This meant that, when the train stopped, one of us would crawl under the car and with his pick start breaking the floor in the two farthest corners from the sliding doors. Although the floor was made of lumber about two inches thick, once a hole was made about a foot square, the dry coal came falling out, and then all we needed to do was to crawl underneath the car and keep pushing the coal from under the car into the pits below. This was, of course, much easier than shoveling the coal from inside the car out the doorway, especially with a larger car, in which it was necessary for us to relay the coal to unload. Needless to say, unloading the coal in this manner damaged the car, and repair was required before it could be used again. The Russian foreman did not allow us to poke holes, but more often than not he ignored us. After all, it was to his advantage, too, if we did our work "efficiently."

Unloading coal cars was brutal. I was amazed that, with our tired and hungry bodies, we could work so hard on this task. When we finished the job, our faces and clothing were covered with coal dust and black soot. Dragging myself back to camp, I could barely carry my tools back to the shed.

Contrary to handling coal, unloading food trains was considered a most desirable job. The men who were assigned to work on the food cars stole vegetables, grain—whatever the load happened to be. Once, when I was recruited for this job, the load was a car of sugar. I was surprised when one of the prisoners asked the Russian guard to open the gunny sack. He took his bayonet and slashed it open. We filled our pockets and gave the helpful guard his share of sugar, too, filling a small bag we made from the original sack. The loot we brought back to the barracks was rarely shared with anyone else. Lured by guesses that there might be some more food trains the following day, the senior soldiers who were most reluctant to volunteer for anything did speak up and offer their services for the next day. As the freight turned out to be as inedible as coal, they returned to the barracks angry and disgusted, a scene the recruits enjoyed secretly.

Most of us worked on an eight-hour shift as we continued with various odd jobs. The men who unloaded trains were, however, on a twelve-hour shift with a twenty-four-hour break in between. I remember the weary look on their faces as they walked around with shovels on their shoulders, ready to go to work the moment a train pulled in with all sorts of freight, most of it heavy and hard to handle. The twelve-hour shift was indeed the worst of all assignments.

One night late in November, some hundred men were called to do extra work, and I was one of them. None of us had any idea what the work would be when we left the camp. Grabbing shovels at the tool shed, we began to march in a direction we had not been before. After what seemed an hour, we saw high banks on both sides. The coal crunched under my boots as we kept walking. It was a coal yard. Suddenly bright orange flames flickered ahead of us. "Wonder what's up?" I said aloud. The Japanese in command yelled, "Spread out. Our task is to extinguish this fire. Use your shovel, and throw dirt on it."

The men fell out of file and moved in the direction of the fire. As far as I could see, no one was trying to put out the fire. What could be better than having a fire on a cold night like this? A Russian foreman came by and started cursing and yelling at the top of his voice. Although we knew he was telling us to shovel dirt on the fire, we did otherwise, as if we didn't understand him. The Russian grabbed my shovel away from me and began throwing dirt on the burning coal. "Like this, like this!" he shouted and threw the shovel back at me. No sooner had I picked up the shovel and begun moving than the prisoner next to me whispered, "Hey, you're going to put out the fire. Just make sure the 'dirt' you shovel is not dirt." The Russian tried now to get the next group down the line to put out the fire. We could hear his shouting and cursing as he continued down the line. After two hours, we walked back to the barracks, leaving the fire burning more strongly than before.

10. Hunger: The Real Enemy

Perpetual hunger was a fact of life in the camp. It was not the Russians' way of mistreating their prisoners but was caused by a severe lack of food for all, including the captors themselves. I saw cartons of dehydrated eggs and gold-colored canned goods with MADE IN U.S.A. and FOR THE ALLIED POWERS stamped on them in black letters. My guess was that they were sent to this country during the war when the Russians were fighting in Europe.

When meals were brought in wooden buckets from the mess hall by younger prisoners assigned to this extra task, all the hungry eyes glistened, trying to detect the slightest sign of uneven serving as the food was divided into plates and bowls lined up at the foot of the bunks. Although dividing anything was touchy, slicing bread in exactly equal portions was nearly impossible. Everyone wanted the heel slice of a loaf. After all, the crusty portion was chewier and gave us more satisfaction than the soft middle portion. I often thought wistfully of the sandwiches my mother in California made when I was a child and how I tore off the crust and tossed it away, eating only the fluffy portion in the middle. The meals here often consisted of steamed buckwheat, rye, or oats, grains considered to be fit only for livestock feed in Japan. We ate them without complaining and even preferred them to rice, which, to our disappointment, had the consistency of porridge as it was cooked with too much water to stretch the small ration to feed many.

The barracks were so poorly lit that it was hard to see what we were eating. This, of course, was a minor problem as it took us but a very short time to wolf down our meager meal. An oil lamp was lit in dark corners during meals, which helped those of us whose bunks were in the corners. In earlier days in the camp, the meal servers purposely left food stuck to the inside of the buckets so that they could scrape it off and eat it before washing them. They did not, however, enjoy this special "benefit" very long. Soon the senior prisoners caught on, and the buckets were inspected to see if they were scraped clean at the time food was distributed.

The different shapes and sizes of plates and bowls did not help the matter, either. "Hey, you guys," grumbled Kondo, who was becoming increasingly greedy and more difficult when the food was divided. "Did you ever take the trouble to measure the plates to see just how much each would hold? And that's not all. You think I didn't know, but you guys cut the bread, trying to make as many crumbs as possible, so you can eat them. From now on, you'd better share the crumbs, too." One day soon after that, we held a squad meeting and decided to measure each eating utensil. All plates and bowls were lined up, and a cup of water was poured into each of them to see to what level the water would rise. After this experiment, it was agreed that a shallow flat container appeared to have less in it than a small deeper one when an equal amount of water was poured into it. We even went around to other squads to exchange dishes and bowls so that we could have as many of similar shapes as possible.

These were not the only measures taken in our desperate attempt to even out the servings. At one point, a second-year soldier was appointed "supervisor of meal distribution." He did not last in this job very long, either, as his superior continued to be dissatisfied with the servings and decided that he was not doing a good job. Someone else's serving always looked bigger, a classic example of grass being greener on the other side of the fence.

It was my turn to be one of three servers one day. Annoyed

with Kondo's constant criticisms and grumbling, I blurted out, "You get down off that bunk and see how well you can handle it." I was aware that it was a big mistake for anyone to talk to Kondo in this manner, but it was too late now. My explosion was triggered not only by his complaints about the food. I was about to burst with a pent-up resentment toward this man who, as our group leader at work, often left us in the cold and found himself some place warm to stay until the time came for us to return to the camp. "Ah, wise guy, eh! OK, you can reduce Suzuki's meal. Give him only half his share of the bread and everything else," he ordered one of the fellow servers. There was nothing I could do. Yasunaga and Kato were punished in the same way for various reasons. I knew Kondo wanted to put as many as he could on half ration so that he himself would get most of what he took away from them. Of course, having our ration reduced to half did not mean that our work load would also be reduced. We still did our regular work plus all the extra chores back in the barracks.

When I went out to throw the dishwater away that night, I saw two dark figures moving about near the warehouse. The next morning we learned that some prisoners had broken into the warehouse and stolen four loaves of bread. The Soviet camp authorities discovered the theft and stopped the ration of bread altogether for the remainder of the week for the entire camp. It was bad enough with the regular ration, which was already meager, but now, without bread for three days, the prisoners' morale sank lower than ever before.

After supper one night, Yasunaga came to me and whispered, "I've found a place where we can get something to eat." We both looked around to make certain that we were not heard. "Follow me and make sure that Bully Kondo doesn't see us," he added. We left the barracks, announcing that we were going to the latrine. (As the youngest of the prisoners, we were still expected to announce our every move as we did in our army days.)

Despite the cloudy and moonless sky, the light around the guard towers and the snow on the ground made the night seem brighter. I followed Yasunaga, as we walked toward the newly constructed barn where the camp kept its horses. "I know this fellow who's taking care of the horses. He's from my parents' hometown in southern Japan," said Yasunaga as we walked around to the back where a dim light was coming through a small window. Yasunaga tapped on the window pane, and a voice from inside answered, "Who's there?" "It's me, Yasunaga. Have you got something for me tonight?" "Come on in," invited the voice from within. The hinges squeaked as we opened the small door and walked in.

The barn was dimly lit with only one small light hanging from the underside of the roof. "This is Suzuki," Yasunaga introduced me to the man. "Bully gave him the half ration, too." Yasunaga's friend, who was much older than we were, nodded silently and motioned for us to follow him to a corner, where there were four large barrels filled with cabbage stems and partially rotten potatoes. We began sorting them and filled our pockets with relatively "good" discards. We then went into the small room located in one corner of the barn where this man slept at night. A warm fire was burning in the *pechika* (the Manchurian brick stove). Chewing the cabbage stems, we sliced off the rotten parts of the potatoes and threw the rest into the fire. "Good, isn't it?" said Yasunaga, visibly enjoying the cabbage, "I know I'd never have thought of eating anything like this, but what else can we do?" I never dreamed of eating horse feed, either. But the cabbage stems and discarded potatoes were delicious, indeed, to the starving prisoners that we were.

Savoring the cooked potatoes, Yasunaga and I talked about a sad and amusing experience I had had. The winter days were short, and by the time we had finished our day-shift work and returned to camp, it was already dark. The spotlight that glared down on us as we entered the gate gave us the eerie feeling of being watched while we could not see who was watching us. The ground was covered with a thin layer of frozen snow. As our group came marching in through the gate five abreast, I saw

some men ducking down ahead of me. The prisoner next to me said, "Look, frozen potatoes on the ground! Must've fallen off the cart when they were bringing in the supply to the camp." I picked up two or three dark lumps, not missing a stride, as I marched toward the barracks with the group.

Once inside, we dashed to the coal-burning *pechika*, which had a metal plate cover two feet square on it. The men gathered around trying to dry their damp boots, socks, and gloves. Some were heating canteens of water, while a few lucky ones put the potatoes they had picked up that evening on the plate to cook. I, too, placed my precious cold, hard lumps on the hot plate and watched them cook. As the heat of the *pechika* thawed them, my "potatoes" began to reveal their true color. They were unmistakably horse dung.

Yasunaga and I had a big laugh over this tragicomedy, munching on the real potatoes in the dark barn. We thanked the caretaker and left. Outside, Yasunaga told me to rub my face with the snow lest the black charcoal marks should give us away when we returned to the barracks. It was the first night in months that I felt I had something in my stomach when I went to bed.

We visited the barn a few more times before the horses were taken away from the camp. The departure of the horses meant we lost the source of discarded vegetables on which we had come to depend so much to ease the pain of hunger. The future looked bleak. I thought about the loss for a long time.

I was getting weaker from the shortage of food, the cold weather, and the hard labor. In the earlier days, I easily carried a bucket of water in each hand in order to cut the number of trips I had to make to the water station, a small white structure with only a single window and a door. It was located near the gate and was our sole source of hot and cold running water in the camp, except for the mess and the dispensary. I was no longer able to carry two buckets of water and was finding it difficult to manage even one. At work outside the camp, the prisoners would trot the last several yards in order to get to the tool shed before the others to get the earlier and better pick of the tools. I was now unable to dash toward the shed like the others and had no choice but to pick up whatever tool was left, and that meant the heavier and more undesirable ones. Try as I may, my legs would not respond. It was as though they were not a part of my body.

One night I noticed that my hands and legs were swollen, but I did not mention it to anyone. Soon my face, too, became puffy, and I had difficulty keeping my eyes open. Walking became difficult, and my boots felt as though they weighed a ton. Returning from work a few days later, I stumbled and fell along the downhill road outside the gate and could not get up. Ohta and another prisoner walking beside me helped me up, put my arms around their shoulders, and carried me back to camp. That night, Bully dragged me out in the aisle of the barracks and slapped me till I fell on my back. My glasses fell off and broke. He was very tall for a Japanese and burly, too. He picked me up again and, holding me by my collar from behind, snarled, "Look at this guy! He doesn't want to work, so he fakes an act. He's eating just like the rest of us but doesn't wanna do his share of the work." He beat me till I lost consciousness. Later, Ohta told me that he could see by the way my eyes looked that something was very wrong. My eyes were wide open but glazed. As Bully let go of his hold, I fell to my knees on the floor between the bunks. Yasunaga came from his bunk to help me up, but Bully said coldly, "Leave him there! Can't you see, he's only faking all this?" The prisoners were hesitant to help, especially if they had to argue with Bully about it. I fell on my face and was left there.

A while later, Ohta and Yasunaga came out and carried me to my bunk. Later that night, I got up and went out of the barracks to the latrine, not fully conscious of what I was doing. Outside, I stumbled and fell in the path. Neither the snow nor the piercing wind could bring me to. It was my good fortune that the night was very cold and many prisoners needed to visit the latrine. Ohta went out, too, and found me lying in the snow. He immediately carried me back into the barracks. My fingertips and toes were frostbitten and were as white as wax. "Hey, Yasunaga, Kato," called out Ohta. "Get up! Come here quick! Suzuki's out. Help me rub his fingers and toes." The two prisoners got up from their bunks, and knelt on the floor where Ohta had put me, and began to rub my frostbitten hands and feet vigorously in the palms of their hands. In the commotion, other prisoners also got up and came over to help.

Bully climbed down from his upper bunk, too, and was now standing behind Ohta. Ohta turned around and said, "You said Suzuki was faking his condition at work and back here at the barracks this evening, but anyone could tell that something was wrong." Bully stood there and said nothing. Although Ohta was fully aware that Bully was his superior and that a subordinate would not talk in this manner normally, he went on, "His swollen face is a clear sign of malnutrition. I think you should be more careful. I don't agree that you have the right to take away any food from any of the men. After all, we are all together in this terrible situation and should help each other survive the best we can." Bully was trembling, but whether from anger or fear, no one could tell. He turned around and climbed back up into his bunk.

Ohta, Yasunaga, and two other prisoners carried me to the dispensary as soon as they saw the color return to my hands and feet. As they walked into the dispensary, Ohta said in a loud voice, "Help us! Please help us!" "What's up?" asked a medic as he came into the waiting room. Ohta explained the situation. The Japanese doctor came into the room and took one look at me and instructed them to take me into the ward and put me down immediately on a bed. "Doctor, look, the guy's nostrils are quivering!" said the medic. "Yes, I see. Doesn't look good at all," said the doctor. "There isn't much else we can do for him, but I want you to keep giving him camphor injections. Here, I'll write it down." The doctor looked at Ohta and the other three men who helped him carry me in and said, "Thank you for doing your part. We'll do all we can for him. What company and squad is he from?" Ohta gave him the information, and the four went out the door.

I finally regained consciousness early in the afternoon of the next day. I opened my eyes and saw Yasunaga sitting beside my bed. I did not fully recognize him and asked, "Where am I? Am I in America? Where is this?" Yasunaga was surprised and somewhat frightened by my remarks and dashed out of the ward to find a medic. He soon returned with the doctor. He put his hands on my forehead as if to check my temperature. He looked at Yasunaga and said something. I closed my eyes and went back to sleep.

A week went by before I could sit up and have my meals. Yasunaga came by often and not only fed me but even took care of my bedpan. I was recovering satisfactorily from symptoms of malnutrition and regaining my strength. Each morning the Russian medical officer came into the room and with the Japanese doctor examined each patient. Twice a day the medic went around the ward to hand each patient a thermometer to check his temperature. I soon learned that having a fever was about the only symptom the Russians recognized and accepted as a sign of an illness. Because of this, the most unfortunate patients were those who had rheumatism. The Russians could not understand what was wrong with the limping men and ordered them out of the dispensary and sent them back to work. There were, of course, some prisoners who pretended to suffer from rheumatism to avoid going to work.

The year 1945 was drawing to a close, and it looked as though I was going to greet the New Year in bed. I knew that I was much better off than some of the other patients around. There was a man suffering from an extreme case of malnutrition who had the bed next to mine. This young man was getting weaker each day. It was New Year's Eve when he began to cry out, "Help, help! I'm cold. What are you doing to me, making me stand out in the cold with nothing to wear?" Two medics on the dispensary staff ran into the ward and strapped him down to the bed. The screaming grew louder and kept up all night. When the thermometers were passed out the next morning, the man was motionless. He was dead. Informed of his death, men from his squad came immediately to carry him away.

I later learned that this man and all the others who died in camp were taken to a nearby cemetery and buried. In the earlier days of our imprisonment, coffins were made for each dead prisoner, and special Japanese sweets were prepared as an offering. A makeshift Buddhist altar was constructed where prayers were said by the surviving prisoners from the same squad. These traditional rituals that the prisoners had known all their lives still had an important place in their minds. Soon, however, all formalities were abandoned. There were reports that the sweets were stolen almost as quickly as they were placed at the altar. In lieu of a tombstone, a plain stick with a number on it was put in the ground for each of the dead. There was no name or any other identification. I recalled the day we cremated Saito back in Manchuria. His death was no more significant than the deaths here; we just found ourselves with too little energy to give much thought to anything except food and work, work and food.

It was New Year's Day 1946. The shortage of food was worse than we had ever seen since arriving at Krasnoyarsk. The cases of malnutrition increased steadily. The disabled prisoners continued to pour into the dispensary, filling every available bed. When I was carried into the dispensary, the facilities occupied only half a barracks, but the separating wall had to be removed to make room for more new patients. The dispensary, double in size now, was filled to capacity.

By April, I was feeling much better, and I began to gain weight. No doubt I would soon have to leave this life and would be sent back to work again. While lying in bed one day, I thought about the book *All Quiet on the Western Front*. In the book, one of the soldiers wishing to be removed from the front lines bribed the doctor and even set a burning match to the thermometer to make it appear as if he had a fever. There was a *pechika* in the ward exactly like those in the other barracks. One day, when Yasunaga came to visit me, I asked him to bring me my canteen. I filled the canteen with water. I woke up at three or four in the morning, quietly got out of bed, took the canteen over to the *pechika*, and left it on the steel plate with the cap off. By the time I got up in the morning, the water was hot. I put the cap back on and brought it back to bed with me.

At six o'clock each morning, the medics came around with thermometers on their regular routine check. As one of them handed me one, I put it under my arm, but as soon as he left the room, I took the thermometer out and placed it beside the canteen under the blanket. I watched closely as the mercury climbed. "*Oops!*" I thought, "that's too much 'fever.'" I took the thermometer out from under the blanket and shook it down to 100°F. I put the thermometer back under my arm and lay still. When the medic came back to check my temperature, I watched him nervously to see if there was any change in his expression. "Fever, 100°F," he said as he read the thermometer. "Safe," I said to myself, greatly relieved that he did not suspect anything. I played this trick twice daily. I was always very careful not to let the mercury go up too high in order to maintain a "slight fever."

One day I saw the Russian medical officer and the Japanese doctor discussing something, occasionally looking toward me. They came over to my bed and told me to take off my shirt. The Japanese doctor took out his stethoscope and ran it over my back. He shook his head and asked me if there was anything wrong. "Can't sleep at night. Every evening I have a headache," I answered. I was certain that the Japanese doctor suspected that the daily record of my temperature was not correct. The two said nothing and moved on to the next patient. I knew the Japanese doctor chose to ignore the discrepancy so that I could stay and rest a little longer in the dispensary. He was a man of compassion and, like a family physician, gave much personal attention to his patients.

One evening the doctor dropped in and said, "I hear you're smoking now. I'm disappointed in you after all I have done to save your life. Smoking isn't good for your condition, you know." Looking sad, he turned away and left. The same doctor had the respect and trust of the Russian medical staff, and his decisions prevailed in most instances. I heard different stories about other camps where the Russians diagnosed all cases and made all decisions concerning patients while the Japanese doctors were mere puppets.

That same evening, Yasunaga paid me another visit and asked how my plan was working. "Just today the doctor asked me if there was anything wrong," I told him. Yasunaga mused, smiling, "Heck, it's all right. You're not cheating anybody but the Russians. It's better to stay here as long as you can, and, besides, there are rumors going around that the Russians are going to release the patients and send them back to Japan very soon."

As time went on, the weather became warmer and more tolerable. Soon I noticed that the *pechika* was not burning regularly. It was about time, I told myself, to stop heating the canteen and the thermometer. Three days later, after more than five months in the dispensary, I was released and sent back to the barracks.

During my absence, a number of changes had taken place. Drastic changes were made in the work groups, with almost everyone now working in the factory. The greatest change was the way in which everyone was being treated more equally. Even the older prisoners now did their share of work, such as bringing the food from the mess and serving it. I also noticed that the prisoners were now addressing one another as "So and So–san" or "Mr. So and So." The old Japanese Army ranks had been abandoned and the grade insignias removed.

11. *The* Otakebi
(Brave Cry) Incident

The routine we went through daily was a constant reminder that we were indeed prisoners of war. The meager supply of food, the poor accommodations, and the barren environment combined to send us into deep depression. The steel bar clanged at 6:00 A.M. now, signaling the time for prisoners to get out of bed, and again at 6:45, when we were to prepare to leave the barracks. We were now merely a moving mass of flesh that was fast deteriorating from malnutrition and the general strain of life in captivity.

The Japanese in command at the camp, a major, was a quiet man in his early forties, with a neatly kept mustache and a deformed hand, perhaps the result of a wound he had suffered in some military operation. I heard he was formerly the commander of a tank unit in the Kwantung Army. Although he kept himself aloof and seldom spoke with the rank and file, it was evident that he cared deeply about the men under his command; every morning he would stand at the gate to see the groups leave for work. As the days went by, the major became more concerned about the lack of food and the sinking morale among his men. Fully aware of the annoyance he would cause our captors, he went to them frequently to describe the plight of his men and negotiated with them fruitlessly for an increase in the food ration. In the absence of recreational facilities and any material to stimulate the minds of his men in the camp, he proposed that all those interested might summon their talent to write a novel or a poem, draw a picture, or compose a song. His proposal contained one grave but unforeseen error, that all the contributions have as their underlying theme "the spirit of the reconstruction of the Japanese empire."

As the invitation to participate in this activity was announced in each barracks, many men dug into their bags to take out writing paper and pencils, which they had forgotten they still possessed. After a day's work at the factory and their all too meager supper, the men gathered under the dim light to work on their projects. Many gave up in the first few days. For those who stayed on the task, the efforts at night in the poorly lit barracks were not enough. They stole a few moments to write during the day when they were in charge of cleaning the barracks or when they were on the night shift. Several weeks went by before the completed works were collected and made into a book crudely bound with a piece of string. Although only a handful of men actually contributed to the collection, the book turned out to be sizable and was passed around among all the barracks. Many prisoners read it with great interest, while some paid little attention to it.

It was only a few weeks into the new year of 1946 when the incident occurred. The barracks were inspected frequently by Russian medical officers, nurses, and camp authorities. One such visitor was a Mongolian-Russian woman who not only spoke Japanese fluently but had knowledge of the written language. As she was walking through the barracks on this day, together with three Russians, she observed a prisoner sitting on the lower level of one of the bunks, reading what looked like a sizable book. It was our "anthology." She approached the man, took her hand from her coat pocket, held it out, and asked for the book. On the cover was written *Otakebi* (brave cry) in large letters. She flipped through the pages, closed the book, and stood there staring into the face of the man.

Expecting that she would return the book to him, he reached out his hand. The woman did not move, still casting a cold, piercing gaze on him. She turned with the book in her hand and walked away with the other three. That evening, several men were called to the Russian camp headquarters, including the commander with the mustache, his assistant, the man who wrote the novel *Otakebi*, the one who had been found reading the book, and his squad leader. As the ranking officer of the barracks, Lieutenant Sasaki was among them. Some said they were moved to Camp 7, which, rumor had it, detained war criminals. Others speculated that they were tried and sentenced to twenty-five years of hard labor, the heaviest sentence for any crime in the Soviet Union besides the death penalty, we were told. Who would know? We were never to see or hear from them again.

I had been ill and was convalescing in the dispensary when this incident occurred and only heard about it from my friend Ohta when he came to visit me. "Boy, weren't you lucky you weren't involved in it!" said Ohta, with a big sigh of relief, for he knew I had worked on some pictures that I had intended to submit for inclusion in the book. Drawing pictures was a modest talent I had, one that had been cultivated when I was a small child. After fights I had with my brother, which often left me crying, my father would have me sit by him and would show me how to draw pictures. I remember him to be quite good at it, and he taught me well. When the invitation for contributions to the book was announced, I started on some pictures, most of which poked fun at Russian soldiers. One depicted a Russian soldier using his bayonet in a melon field to pierce a melon and toss it in the air. At that time, the idea of a soldier using his weapon for such antics was unpardonable in the eyes of a Japanese soldier, and the caption written under the picture belittled the Russian soldier for doing this. I had become ill before finishing the drawings and was sent to the dispensary. "Just think if you had submitted something and had gotten in that thing!" Ohta could not get over my incredible good fortune.

With hindsight, one can easily see how foolish and dangerous it was for us to put down our thoughts in writing, let alone the thought of rebuilding Japan as an empire. I look back on the incident with sadness and amazement at our naïveté and ignorance. At that time, especially in the early months of our captivity, we were quite oblivious to the consequences of such an activity. The Japanese soldier was never taught or trained what action to take as a prisoner other than to take his own life. To live on in captivity was simply not in the realm of possibility to the Imperial Japanese Army.

The incident was another rude awakening to a harsh reality.

12. Factory Work: Fooling the Boss

Ohta was no longer in our squad when I was released from the dispensary. He had been transferred to the camp headquarters, where his special talent for figures and organization was put to good use. I heard he was the one who had saved my life six months before when I was very ill and fell unconscious in the snow. Anxious to tell him how indebted I was to him, I visited the headquarters and found him working behind a large desk. "Are you busy? I got back to my group today and will have to start going to work tomorrow. I heard all about the way you saved my life, and I want to thank you," I said as I approached the desk, hoping I was not interrupting his work. Ohta looked up and smiled, visibly pleased to see me in better shape than I was when he last saw me. He said, "You did have a close call. You know, we all thought you were a goner. Is everything all right?" "Yes, my legs feel a little weak, but I think I'll be all right," I replied as I sat down on the bench in front of his desk.

Ohta got up and went over to his bunk and came back with a package of tobacco. "Here, you smoke, don't you?" he asked, offering me a fistful of loose tobacco. "Yes, thank you, thank you very much," I said, and took a sheet of folded newspaper from my pocket. I tore off a piece to roll a cigarette as the Russians did. The Russians carried loose tobacco in their pockets or in small bags. They also carried with them regular newspapers, which they folded neatly into small squares. They tore the paper straight along the crease of the fold and rolled the tobacco into cigarettes. It was quite a skill, which fascinated the Japanese, who were unfamiliar with rolling their own cigarettes. The flint we used was a light-gauge pipe about six inches long with a piece of cotton wick through it. We used a piece of file to strike against the flint stone to light the wick. After lighting the cigarette, we simply pulled in the wick and put it away in our pocket. I borrowed a flint from Ohta and lit the cigarette. Watching me, Ohta said, "You're getting pretty good. I'd sure like to show the people back home how things are done over here," laughing in his high-pitched voice. He continued, "You've heard about all the changes and the different sort of work we're doing nowadays, too, haven't you?" I nodded and took a deep puff. It was sweet, just as I heard people say about the Russian tobacco.

Ohta, too, lit a cigarette and began, "There's a new group that was organized only a few days ago. The group works at the foundry. You have no experience, I'm sure, but I think you can go there and work. I hear the work isn't very heavy, and, besides, it'll be warm in winter. Of course, we don't expect to be here another winter, but who knows? . . . I personally think it'll be the best place for you—so if you'd like, I'll be able to get you in that group." He went on, "It may, however, take a few days until I process the papers for you, so I suggest you go to a small group that's working in the paint shop until then. I hear the Japanese leaders at both of these places are very understanding people. I'm sure you'll find it to be quite a change from your days before. I'll do whatever I can to keep you away from Bully."

I thanked Ohta for the help. We talked for nearly an hour, about the past we shared, the present, and the future, especially the future and our hopes of going home soon. "I hear that the Russians are saying nowadays, 'Soon you'll return,' whenever we ask them, 'When do we leave? When do we leave?' And you know how often we ask them that question," said Ohta, but then a sudden shroud of anxiety and doubt clouded his face, as he added, "Don't forget, though, how they handled us when they brought us over here. Sort of strung us along, don't you think?"

The next morning I left the barracks at the familiar sound of the steel bar and lined up with my new group, Group 15, in front of the gate. Group 15 was a group of only six men. Even the guard seemed friendlier, although he had, as did the previous guards, an automatic rifle strapped over his shoulder. Walking with the group toward the factory, I recalled Ohta describing how I had been carried over this same road back to the camp when I was so weak I stumbled and fell in the snow.

As we entered the factory gates, I saw another group of prisoners unloading a flatcar. I immediately spotted Bully, who was working right along with the rest. What a change! He was no longer standing with his hands on his hips giving out orders. Although it was difficult for me to forget his cruelty, I felt pity for him, as I could see how thin and wan he was and how weak he seemed now.

We arrived at the paint shop. The walls were about twenty feet high with glass panes in the top half. The floor was concrete, and there were small rooms in one corner of the structure. As we stood there, the large sliding door at one end opened, and a small truck came through, pulling behind it three trailers. Each trailer had four wheels, and on it was mounted an antiaircraft gun. Our work was to unhook the trailer from the truck, disconnect the trailers from each other, then push them to the painting area. There they were spray-painted by the Russian workers, after which we pushed each trailer into one of the small rooms in the corner, which were drying ovens. The work was simple, and since the wheels were inflated rubber tires, the trailers glided on the smooth floor. Adjacent to the paint shop was a machine shop, where we went after putting all the trailers into the ovens to do cleanup work, such as removing the metal shavings from around the machine and sweeping the floor. There was no comparison between all this easy work and the digging of trenches or unloading of the freight cars that we had done before. The Russian workers around us were quite friendly and often stopped us to make conversation. Although I was unable to communicate much with them, I managed with much gesticulation and a very limited vocabulary to make them understand what I did in Japan before I was recruited into the army as well as a few other subjects.

My work at the paint shop came to an abrupt end on the second day. It was close to noon when several Russian officers visited the shop. The ranking officer must have been a general, for his lapel was a field of gold. Pointing toward us and waving his arms, he looked back over his shoulder and shouted something to the other officers around him. We had just maneuvered a trailer into one of the ovens and were standing around to watch them. We looked at each other and whispered, "What the heck is that all about?" As the noon whistle blew, we were ordered to gather and prepare to return to camp. As we went out one door with our friendly guard, I saw the Russian officers and the angry general walking out the other door.

Heading back toward camp, I saw our leader talking with the guard and soon learned that all the commotion and our sudden return to camp were caused by fear on the part of the Russians that the prisoners, if interested, would be able to have an accurate count of the number of antiaircraft guns being produced at this factory during an eight-hour work shift. On our arrival back at the camp, we were officially notified that Group 15 was to disband. We spent the rest of the day doing cleanup work within the camp.

Ohta dropped by our barracks that evening and invited me to visit him at his office after supper. While standing in the corridor below the bunks, Ohta looked up and greeted Bully, no longer the burly man that he had been, having lost much weight. "How is work, Kondo-san? I understand you're on the twelve-hour shift. It's pretty rough, isn't it? Hope you'll take care of yourself," said Ohta, looking at the former sergeant with sympathy. Bully sounded lethargic. "I'm on the damn night shift now and so must be leaving soon."

Ohta informed me that evening that he had completed the paperwork for me and that I would therefore be expected at the foundry the next day as a member of Group 21.

The following day, I left the camp with my new group. On arriving at the factory, we dispersed to do various jobs there. I followed Ishikawa to one corner of the building to work with the machine that made tracks for army tanks. Our work team consisted of two Russian women, Ishikawa, and me. The two of us stood behind the machine and shoveled sand into the frame. Ishikawa then pulled the lever, which brought the second frame down on the first, and turned the two frames over where the women were positioned. After leaving the frames there, the rack returned to its original position. We placed another set of frames on the rack and repeated the process, while the women workers put the finishing touches on the mold. That was all there was to my new work at the foundry. "Certainly one doesn't need any experience for this," I thought to myself, much relieved. The rack swung back and forth between us and the women as we continued our work.

At the sound of the whistle signaling our lunch break, the women threw down their tools and began eating, even though a few more strokes of their spatulas would have completed the mold. They seemed even more eager to drop their work and get to their lunch when they had just received their pay. It was apparent that these two women were not the ones to push us to produce more work as we worked as a team. This was quite a contrast to my other experiences, in which the Russian foremen pushed us constantly with their *Bystryey, bystryey!* (Hurry, hurry!) and *Lapota, lapota!* (Work, work!).

Working with these women gave me the first chance to actually see what the Russians were eating. For lunch they usually brought a hunk of bread about the size of a fist and a piece of rock salt. They took a bite of the bread, then licked the piece of salt, and then had two bites of the bread. They walked over to the faucet to drink water after they finished their bread. As the months went by, their lunch did improve. Although their bread was the same black, hard sour bread, a small bottle of milk replaced water, and a little dab of butter or a small piece of meat was added in place of salt. I realized that the prisoners' food ration did not compare too poorly with the captors' diet.

The whistle blew again, and we resumed work for the afternoon. The electric furnace and the gas furnace began to roar. Overhead the cranes were swinging back and forth. It took several days before I became accustomed to the high noise level and was able to concentrate on my work. Ordinarily, we kept pace with the women comfortably. Or it may have been the other way around. Often it appeared that they worked hard to keep up with us. There were times, however, when neither Lever-man (Ishikawa) nor I was in the mood for much work. We would then come up with ways to stall things. The frames were delivered to our machine by a crane, which was operated by a fellow prisoner. When we were not that eager to work, we did not call the crane for delivery of a new supply of empty frames, which made it necessary for the women to call for the crane themselves. As we saw the crane approach us, we yelled in Japanese, "Hey, don't come this way. We don't need you!" The crane driver knew what we were up to and drove away. The women would then ask, "What did you tell him?" "Nothing, nothing important. We just told him to hurry and bring us some more empty frames," replied Lever-man. "Oh no you didn't. You chased him away," the women chided, although they too did not mind an occasional break in their work. The argument usually did not go beyond that.

Another scheme of ours to stall the work involved causing an air leak in the machine so that the rack did not move. One day the machine broke down, and the maintenance man was called in immediately. As the man worked on the machine, Lever-man stood by to hand him the necessary tools and help him out generally. No one knew what he was up to as he worked alongside the Russian repairman. Lever-man took mental notes of how the machine was put together so that he might be able to use that knowledge at some later time when we wanted a slowdown.

The machine did "break down" twice in the same week sometime after that, and each time the repairman was called back. His boss came with him the second time. From the tone of his voice and the way the maintenance man was responding, we gathered that the boss was blaming him for the poor repair work he was doing. We also surmised that the repairman was saying we had something to do with the breakdown, as he kept pointing in our direction. The boss turned toward us and asked something in Russian. Although we hardly knew the language, we knew he was asking whether we indeed had had something to do with the trouble. We tried our best to look puzzled and innocent and protested, "Don't know, don't know. Lots of work, lots of bread," shrugging our shoulders. We were unaware that what we had done could be considered sabotage. If they decided it was a case of sabotage, the penalty would have been severe. We tried our best to convince them that we could not have possibly attempted to interfere with production, knowing that the more we produced, the more bread we'd be given.

Weeks and months went by, and another summer was on us in this cold Siberia. Unlike in the cold winter months, the walk to and from the factory became pleasant. The grass that sprang forth from the ground in a short period of time took me back to the summer in Manchuria before Japan's surrender, when a sudden burst of plant life lightened the hearts of the men in military training. Any sign of life such as this did wonders for the prisoners, taking them away from the dreariness of the long and cold winter and the thin layer of snow covering the ground month after month.

When our work was lagging one day, Lever-man shared what he had been thinking about lately. He said, "That black liquid they're painting on the surface of the larger molds. . . . I think it's sweet and edible. Next time we get a chance, let's try to boil some in our lunch pail. There was a fellow who used to work in a foundry back in Japan. He said that they used something made from brown sugar for the same purpose. There's a small quantity of mineral oil mixed in this stuff, but I think if we boil it, it'll be safe to eat." At noon we filled our pails with the liquid and put them over a mold that had been cast that morning and was still red hot. The liquid soon began to bubble and boil. After a short period of boiling, we removed the pails from the cast. The whistle blew again to begin the afternoon work. When the liquid cooled off, Lever-man stuck his finger into the pail and licked it. "Sweet," he exclaimed. "I think we got something here." We took what we had made back to camp that evening and put it on a piece of bread. "Hey, this is good! No more shortage of sugar for us!"

The discovery gradually got around to the other groups in the same barracks and then to the entire camp. Soon some of the fast "businessmen" in Group 21 brought back the liquid not only for themselves but to trade for tobacco. When a new supply of the liquid was delivered to the factory, the word got around rapidly, and the entire group, with buckets and other containers, dashed toward the barrel at the noon whistle. If the barrel was in an open area, the crane driven by a prisoner was even called to help. The crane came to the rescue swiftly and carried the barrel to a corner, where the liquid could be taken out of sight of the Russians. However, this operation could not last forever. Soon the factory was out of the liquid constantly, which, of course, hampered the production of the larger molds. The Russian camp authorities were informed of this activity, and the sugar rush of Group 21 came to an abrupt halt, but not soon enough for the men who ate too much of it and became ill.

There was another short-lived, unexpected benefit from working with Group 21. One day the camp mess was ordered by the Russian authorities to construct an oven so that we could bake our own bread. As firebricks were needed for this project, a bulletin was issued that implied that those prisoners connected with the foundry might pilfer and bring back the bricks from the

factory. I recalled the time when Group 1, assigned to construction work, was asked to "supply" lumber and other material to spruce up the camp in preparation for the Great May Day Celebration. This was a similar situation. The camp needed something built, and the prisoners were expected to provide the materials. The reward, it was announced, would be a loaf of bread for every eight bricks delivered.

Lever-man and I talked it over and agreed to carry back four bricks each and split a loaf. During our lunch break, we went to the area where firebricks were stored, took our bricks, and tied a wire around them. Lever-man was well prepared. "Here, take this piece of rag," he said as he tossed the rag over to me. "Wrap it around the wire so it won't dig into your shoulders. It may seem light enough with only two on one shoulder, but by the time we get near the camp, you'll feel it." I did just as I was told, wrapping the piece of rag around the wire. That afternoon, when work was over and we were ready to leave, we all strung our loads over our shoulders and put our overcoats on to cover them. The weather was now warmer, and most of the men on the day shift went to work without their overcoats, but, of course, we came prepared on this occasion to hide our bricks as we walked back to camp. Eight bricks to a loaf of bread was too good a deal to last long. The next day, the value of bricks plummeted to sixteen for a loaf. After the second day, the deal was quickly called off. The mess had all the bricks it needed to complete the oven!

There were other work groups at the factory. Some of them required previous experience, such as lathe operating, auto mechanic work, and welding. The prisoners who had these and similar skills did quite well at their workplaces and were treated especially well by their Russian bosses.

In spite of the fact that hard labor such as unloading the coal cars was still part of our life at the camp, things had improved noticeably compared to the first winter.

13. Boots and Bullies:
A Second Winter in Siberia

The few trees lining the road at the factory were shedding their golden-brown leaves. The fallen leaves danced in the chilly wind until they were dashed against the curb and the sides of the drab buildings. Clearly, summer was over, and autumn seemed to have gone by too swiftly for anyone to notice. Ohta was right, unfortunately, in predicting the possibility of our spending a second winter in Siberia. There was little hope of our returning to Japan until next spring at the earliest. As I looked down from higher ground toward the Trans-Siberian Railroad, which ran between our Camp 5 and Krasnoyarsk Fuji, its tracks looked abandoned, another stark reminder that the possibility of our freedom had disappeared or at least had been suspended until the next spring thaw. Yet we hung on to our hope until the last possible moment, when our fear turned into a confirmed reality by the word spread at work and in the camp. Not having a voice in the decision, we had no choice but to accept the situation, although our disappointment ran much deeper than we dared show. We were too tired to feel bitterness or anger about the dreadful prospect of another Siberian prison camp winter.

The newspaper published in Japanese for the prisoners carried articles on the repatriation of Japanese soldiers. According to these reports, we were to be kept in Siberia for another winter as the Japanese government had its hands full with the problems accompanying surrender. Many soldiers were returning home

from the South Pacific theater just as their homeland was making a desperate attempt to cope with the ravages of the war and
to survive in the face of low energy, low morale, and a severe lack
of material resources. The Japanese government was not eager to
add those of us in Siberia to the number of repatriates from the
south who were pouring in. The optimists among us said they
looked forward to next spring as the time to go home, while
those who were more pessimistic feared that the Russians would
keep us here through the summer to get the most work out of
us and that it would therefore be autumn before we left.

Covered with a thin layer of snow, all in sight was white once
again. As the temperature continued to fall, the snow became a
layer of ice. Contrary to what I had always imagined, there was
relatively little snow in the region of Siberia where we were incar-
cerated. I had seen beautiful pictures of snow country in northern Japan, where the snow would pile up to the eaves of the
houses. I was glad that that was not the case here and that we
were at least spared the task of shoveling snow.

Our barracks were constructed to cope with the icy Siberian
winter. The rows of windows along the sides of the barracks were
equipped with double sashes spaced six inches apart, with sawdust and wood shavings placed at the bottom to absorb the con-
densation. On each end of the barracks was an entrance. The
outside door, covered with gunnysack for added insulation, led
to the entrance hall, eight feet square, and then to the inside
door, which opened into the barracks.

In winter, the perimeter of the interior face of the outer door
was covered with frost as the cold air seeped in and came in contact with the warm air. When the inside door was opened, a gust
of fog created by the cold air encountering the warmer room air
would blow into the barracks. The colder the day, the greater the
fog that blew down the passage between the bunks. The prisoners occupying the bunks near the door often complained about
the frequency of the door opening and closing and yelled at the
users to close the door faster.

This winter, in addition to Japanese Army gear and Russian boots, we were issued two items captured from the German Army. One was a camouflaged windbreaker jacket, the other oversized footwear. The latter, we were told, was worn by the German tank soldiers when they ventured outside the tanks. To be sure, they were large enough to be worn over a regular pair of shoes. The soles were made of wood about an inch thick, and the upper portion was made of a felt-like material with large buckles for fasteners. We abandoned these boots soon; they were almost impossible to walk in even for a very short distance. The wooden sole provided no grip on the slick icy surface. One prisoner, however, wore the footwear rather skillfully. A tall, energetic man named Sato, who drove trucks and was well liked by the Russians, wore the boots as if to show off, waving his arms and declaring that the boots were "OK" with a big grin on his face. The rest of us guessed that he fancied himself as a tank soldier going off to battle. At any rate, we all envied him for his ability to get along with the Russians.

The two most important items for us were footwear and an overcoat. Whenever I saw a Russian soldier standing in the guard tower in his heavy overcoat in weather colder than -60°F or the Russian workers coming to work in the heavy coats that they would take off as soon as they entered the warm building, I was impressed with how well suited those coats were for this bitterly cold Siberian climate. Even more impressive than the overcoats were the Russian boots. Suppose the Japanese Kwantung Army had invaded Siberia. With the kind of boots we had, the casualties from frostbite would have been colossal. On the other hand, some argued, if the Kwantung Army were winning in Siberia, the psychological effect of an offensive might have done something to minimize the casualties, even if the boots were inadequate for the extreme cold of the region.

The Kwantung Army boots had rubber soles and heels with a canvas upper portion, and the insides were lined with rabbit fur. The Russian boots, on the other hand, were made of a felt-like material a quarter inch thick and were molded in one continuous piece with no seam from top to bottom. The sole and heel were also part of that one piece. When the boots were new, the bottom sole section would still be rounded, which caused the wearer to feel as though he were rocking from left to right. They soon flattened out, however, and became perfectly comfortable winter footwear.

One important thing to remember when wearing these boots was to dust off the snow before entering a building. If we did not take time to do this properly, the snow would melt in the warm room, soaking the felt boots. A wet pair of boots worn outside would, of course, freeze immediately and become stiff. It was particularly important for us to keep a watchful eye on our own boots as some men would wear a pair that belonged to someone else to go to the mess or the latrine and would not take the trouble to dust off the snow when they returned. Occasionally, a man was caught taking someone else's shoes, which often resulted in a brawl.

Drying out our boots, stockings, and gloves over the *pechika* in the barracks became a ritual at the end of every work shift during the winter months. It was not always an advantage to have a good pair of boots, either. The prisoners with good boots spent much time taking care of them and were extra careful not to have them stolen by fellow prisoners. At one point, shoe theft occurred so frequently that it became the night watch's duty to make sure that people from other barracks would not enter ours to raid our boots. Some of the more cautious prisoners took their boots to bed with them.

The Russian stockings issued to us, made of a piece of flannel cloth about eighteen inches square, were also quite different from what we had known. We wore them by placing our foot near the center and folding the cloth over and around the foot and ankle. I remembered seeing Russian soldiers with these stockings when we first encountered them on our train ride from Manchuria. I didn't know how they could walk any distance without the stockings coming off and balling up somewhere inside their boots. However, we soon learned that there were advantages to these stockings, as they were easier to wash and dry; they also wore out more evenly as they had no heel or toe.

The men who had lived in Manchuria had good knowledge of the weather cycle on the Asian continent. According to them, three very cold days were usually followed by four days of relatively mild temperatures, and this pattern would repeat itself. Although I didn't know if this cycle could be explained scientifically, it did seem that a few days of cold and warmer temperatures arrived alternately. After cold spells when the thermometer registered -60°F or below, the temperature would rise ten or fifteen degrees. The hardier prisoners then unbuttoned and put up the earflaps of their headgear, exposing their ears to the elements.

As we walked to and from our workplace, I was often reminded of the day we arrived at Hailar as young recruits and stomped our feet on the frozen ground to try to keep them warm. How we were yelled at and ridiculed by our superiors. Now it was all permissible. We moved about with our hands in our pockets and were allowed to do almost anything to keep warm. On colder days, we would look into each others' faces on our way to work and warn each other if the tip of the nose had turned white, a sign of frostbite. As soon as this was detected, we rubbed our nose vigorously with the palm of our glove as we walked briskly toward our destination to get the blood circulating once again. After a severe cold spell, there were many peeling noses, a sign that first-degree frostbite had taken its toll.

That winter I was keenly aware of the help I had received from Ohta in getting this work assignment. While others had to work outside or in unheated buildings, inside the foundry I did not need my overcoat unless it was exceptionally cold. The warmth in the building came from the red-hot steel casts placed at strategic locations, making the workplace a completely different world from that I experienced the first winter. On a few days, the temperature dropped so low that the moisture in the air-supply tubes running along the walls froze and blocked the air passage. Our work, then, had to be halted completely, and we were reassigned to other tasks, such as moving the pig iron around or general cleanup. The Russian workers and our foreman showed little enthusiasm for these odd jobs, and, as a result, we prisoners were not pushed to work very hard.

I heard about an incident that occurred at another foundry. One of the Japanese prisoners shoved a Russian guard into the furnace and then threw himself in after the guard. This particular guard was known to be extremely cruel to the prisoners, and the Japanese, no longer able to endure his rough treatment and humiliation, decided to do away with the guard and also to sacrifice himself to draw the attention of the prison authorities to the plight of the prisoners in the hope that conditions would improve for the rest. The purpose was accomplished: Russian guards became less hostile to us than in the earlier days of our captivity. Although I do not know how much of the story of "the sacrificing prisoner" was true, my guess is that it stemmed partly from the virtue of self-sacrifice for a cause that had been drilled into every Japanese soldier.

A small contingent of men numbering around fifty joined our camp after the first winter. The men had worked in the forests farther north, where their task had been to fell trees. Their camp was reportedly much more primitive than ours, without electricity or other facilities, and was located far from their place of work, requiring them to leave early in the morning and walk a long distance to get to work. They were able to meet only 20–30 percent of the quota, we were told, and as a consequence their food ration was reduced to a meager portion, causing half the workforce to die of malnutrition and exhaustion the first winter. A number of prisoners simply dropped dead while working. The corpses were buried under the snow, which was simply scraped aside and later shoveled back on top of them. Although I did not talk personally with any of the prisoners who survived these extremely adverse conditions, it was clear that there were men who suffered a great deal more than some of us from the poor conditions of prison life and the cruelty of the Siberian winter. I again thought about Saito's death at Company Headquarters in Manchuria. I remembered how difficult it was for our leader to inform his parents of the death of their son. Who was to notify the families of all those men who perished in the forest in some far corner of Siberia?

14. From Factory to Farm: Kindness of a Friend

We had endured our second winter in Siberia. Lingering winter 1946 was reluctantly giving way to the signs of spring. The days were getting noticeably longer and warmer. Even with warm clothing and the advantage of our bodies becoming conditioned to the bitter Siberian winter, it was still a tremendous struggle to go about our daily tasks when the thermometer registered -50°F and lower. All outdoor work was halted when the temperature dropped to -40°F. All this was now behind us. Spring arrived! Although we still wore winter outfits, those prized Russian boots were becoming a nuisance as the sun began to melt the icy surface here and there.

One evening after work, Ohta dropped by my barracks. He said casually, "Oh, there you are, Suzuki. How are things going? Why don't you come around to my place once in a while? You know those of us at headquarters don't get to hear all the rumors and gossip you people out at work are able to hear. What are they saying about our chances of being repatriated soon? Can you come over to my place this evening after supper? I'll be waiting." I was puzzled by Ohta's remark that I had not visited him. I had gone there at least once a week, and it was only yesterday that I was there last. But then I remembered that he would always tell me to drop by whenever I ran into him, and, when I did, he would often have a package of tobacco to give to me.

After finishing my meal and chores, I picked up my boots and went out the door. The evening air was icy as I headed toward the headquarters barracks. I looked over to the right and saw in the dim twilight the outline of the latrines to which I was going the night I fell in the snow and lay unconscious, was rescued by Ohta, and carried into the barracks. As I walked on, I thought of his maneuvering to arrange for me to work at more desirable places. "Gosh, am I lucky," I thought to myself as I opened the door and entered the headquarters barracks. I wondered if there was something to the Buddhist belief that life is one continuous cycle and that our experiences in the present life are tied to the relationships and occurrences of the previous life. What was my relationship with Ohta in my last life? I contemplated that as I entered the building.

Not finding Ohta at his bunk, I wandered around and found him at his office. He was busy working on his ledger. Looking up, he said, "You're looking better. I'm sure you are getting used to the work, and with the warmer weather things should keep improving. With the coming of spring, the camp has just been ordered to organize a workforce to be sent to the collective farm." We talked about all the advantages of life on the farm as compared to staying at the factory. Of course, I needed very little persuading, if any. I knew the two men from our adjacent squad who had gone to the farm the previous summer. Although there were Russian soldiers as guards on the farm, too, the openness and "freedom" was undeniably part of life there. "When do I leave?" I asked with excitement and enthusiasm, contrary to my usual reticent way. "Well, as I said," continued Ohta, with a smile on his face and motioning his right hand as if to calm me down, "we just got this order today from the Russians to draw up a list of names. But I think it'll be soon. Last year the men left for the farm in June. Things are better organized now, so I think it should be sometime in May." "Now remember," he cautioned, "don't say too much about this because it's all in the planning stage yet." I thanked him for his continuing help and left his barracks.

As I walked out, I felt the cold air in my face, but I didn't mind it at all. It was no longer cold but felt quite refreshing. If I went to the farm, I'd be able to get away from my old squad leaders, not only during my work hours, but completely. I returned to my barracks, took off my boots at the entry, and went in. It was late, and the barracks was quiet, with just a few men still talking in low voices, as I walked down the passage between the bunks. Bully was snoring up in his bunk when I got back to mine. Now that he has to work like the rest of us, I thought, he doesn't have the energy to visit and talk or play mah-jongg using a set made by some skilled prisoners. Someone from the lower bunk said, "Turn him over on his side so he'll stop snoring." To treat a superior like this was unthinkable a few months ago, but now it was actually happening. As soon as I took off my trousers and shirt and climbed into my bunk, Yasunaga asked, "What's up, Suzuki, anything new?" "Nothing much," I replied. "Ohta wanted to know more about how I was doing, especially about how 'Kondo no Yatsu' [that Bully Kondo] was behaving." "You told him things have changed, I'm sure. Listen to that bastard snore. Can't help but feel a little sorry for him, though, even after all he did to us," said Yasunaga. Although I was excited about the possibility of going to the farm, I soon dozed off.

The days after my last meeting with Ohta dragged by as I anxiously waited for further word on my prospect of being transferred to the farm. One day, finally, the leader of Group 26 approached me and told me that I was to return to camp at noon that day. I knew that the day to leave for the farm had finally arrived. I returned to camp with the Russian guard, whom I left as soon as I entered the gate of the camp, and hurriedly walked to my barracks. I grabbed my few belongings and hurried down the hall toward the door. I looked back over my shoulder, and, during those few brief moments, all that happened to me as a prisoner in these barracks flashed in my mind—the clanging of the metal plates and dishes, the dreaded commands from the

With my brother, Patrick, 1926

My family, 1932. *Back row (left to right)*: Tsuta (mother), Yoneko (sister), Ichizo (father). *Center row*: Florence (sister), myself, Patrick (brother). *Front row*: Roy (brother), Belle (sister)

As a high school student, Tokyo, 1941

Working for the Allied Occupation Forces (with Walter Lindberg), 1949

Working for the Occupation (with Jack Hammond), 1950

At Hakone, Japan, 1951

With my father, 1952

Palo Alto, California, 1996

sergeants, and numerous memories of humiliation and frustration. I asked myself if there were any good memories of this place. Yes, of course. How about the friendships and support of the men with whom I suffered?

The bright noonday sun felt so good as I stepped out of the building. A light-brown-colored former Japanese Army truck was parked in the space in front of the camp gate. It was that happy, enthusiastic driver Sato's high-pitched voice that I heard as I approached the truck. He was challenging a Russian soldier to a wrestling match. There were other men with their gear ready to board the truck. Even with the Russian officers standing around, I couldn't help but feel an atmosphere of anticipation and excitement as if we were preparing to leave on a happy outing. Soon I saw Ohta coming toward us from the headquarters building. He had a sheet of paper in his hand, which he handed over to the Japanese ex-noncommissioned officer standing with the Russian officers. He read the list aloud, and, as our names were called out, we climbed aboard one by one.

I positioned myself in the right rear corner of the truck. Ohta came over and, looking up, said, "Good luck. Take care of yourself. A truck will be going to the farm regularly once a week—so if there's anything you need, make sure to give the message to the driver. Here, take these." He handed me two packages of tobacco and added, "I hear that tobacco is one thing that's difficult to get on the farm." Sato, the driver, had started the engine, and black smoke puffed out of the exhaust pipe. The roar of the motor drowned out my voice as I struggled to find the right words to express my deep feeling of gratitude to Ohta, who had done so much for me. I sat in my corner, waving, as the truck passed through the camp gate. The gate was closed, and I saw Ohta no longer.

From my corner, I looked around for faces I might know and recognized only two or three of the twenty passengers from my days at the malnutrition unit where I stayed very briefly after leaving the dispensary and before returning to my former squad.

With two thousand men in camp and no time or energy for socializing, it was only natural that we did not get acquainted with anyone outside our own squad, or barracks at the most. I said to myself, however, that I preferred being among strangers to living with the likes of Bully.

The truck sped along the bumpy dirt road. The city and factory were fast fading into the distance. We soon came on the Yenisey River. Beyond the river on the opposite bank, situated on a somewhat higher plateau, was what appeared to be an airfield. In my school days in Tokyo, I had an interest in airplanes and subscribed to a monthly aviation magazine. I could identify most of the military planes of the countries at war and therefore was able to recognize the airplanes lined up in the airfield in the distance as American-made Bell P-39 Airacobras. The sleek silhouette with the long nose wheel did not seem to interest anyone else in the truck but me. To see "in the flesh" something I had seen and read about only in books and magazines was thrilling.

Of more interest to each of us was, of course, our present situation. "At least we won't be sleeping behind walls and watchtowers at the farm," someone said. "Yeah, and I hear there are only three Russian soldiers as guards out there," came the reply. With such conversation and the open country around me, I was beginning to feel a little freedom for the first time since coming to Siberia. It was mid-May, and everything around us confirmed that it was springtime. Looking down toward the river, we saw the huge chunks of broken-up ice along the banks. The gray water was making waves and flowing rapidly and freely, as if to suggest the beginning of new life for nature and for us prisoners.

"I wonder how much farther we've got to go," I said to no one in particular. "We should be getting there soon. I'm getting hungry," replied a tall, slim man, sitting in the opposite rear corner of the truck bed, who looked to be in his early forties. He was one of the men whom I had recognized as a former malnutrition patient. "That's one thing we won't have to worry about—food," said the other former malnutrition patient, who

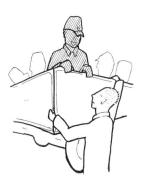

looked about as old as the slim man and whose round face sported a mustache. "We'll get enough to eat on the farm, so I suggest you take heed and watch how much you eat. You need to be careful, you know. Ha ha." "Yeah, I know the dilemma I'm facing," said Slim to Mustache. "I've heard rumors that with the warmer weather they've started working on the 'malnutrition list' for repatriation, and, by golly, I'm going to have to make that one and get back to Japan just as soon as possible. My understanding is that this list will be composed of malnutrition and TB cases."

As I looked around at the others on the truck, I realized for the first time that most of the men were on the fragile side and must have been malnutrition patients at one time or another. Listening to this conversation, I was sure I was not the only one who recognized the dilemma that each of us was facing: being healthy and strong so that work would not be hard, or being weak and unproductive so that the Soviet government would send us home. A long silence followed as we pondered this question.

The truck with its twenty silent passengers continued to speed along the dirt road toward its destination. The scenery along the road suggested that we were nearing our farm. I saw Russian people, mostly children and women and some older men, carrying a bag in one hand and walking the fields looking down. It was not until sometime after arriving at the farm that I heard what these people were doing. The previous winter was a harsh one, and the crop had been exceptionally poor. I heard that even the farmers did not have enough to eat because of the poor harvest and that they were now scrounging around in the fields to pick up the potatoes left in the field over the winter, which were now completely dehydrated and had the appearance of dried prunes that were chalky white in color. These potatoes were picked up and taken home, where the dried skin was scraped off and the pieces put into a pot of water to be cooked. I thought about the food ration back at the camp. How we complained! Yet here were Russians, people who had won the war, picking up "garbage" from the field to eat.

15. Outdoor Interlude: The Collective Farm

The truck made its last turn in the road and finally stopped. We had arrived at our destination. We all stood up at once and climbed out of the truck bed. A Russian sergeant, short in stature, his subordinates, and the ranking Japanese, a noncommissioned officer named Numato, were there to "welcome" us. The Russian sergeant barked out an order. Numato answered, "Yes, this is it, one truckload." The sergeant again said something in a loud voice, waving his arm. Driver Sato yelled out, "Line up, you guys. The sergeant wants you to line up. He wants to count you guys." "Yes, yes, line up so that the sergeant can count you," parroted Numato. We all fell in line. Sergeant Short walked in front of us and began his count, "One, two, three . . . twenty. Good, all here." "Twenty, good!" said spineless Numato, parroting again. Driver Sato was saying something to the Russian private. From his gesture, I could only make out that he was referring to Spineless, his inability to understand Russian, and his total subordination to Sergeant Short.

I looked around the farm compound and found that all the structures were built partially buried, with only half the walls and the roofs above ground. Driver Sato had parked his truck at one end of the compound. To the right was a structure about twelve feet square. This was the mess-kitchen, where the cook also slept. To the left were two rows of structures about thirty feet in length and sixteen feet wide. These were the barracks, where we were to have our bunks. Unlike the setup at the main camp, the bunks were not tiered. They were arranged along both walls with a passageway between them. There was only one small window at either end of the barracks. The floor was dirt, and the bunks were one continuous platform about a foot off the floor. There was a space at the foot of each bunk for our personal belongings. Situated between our barracks and the mess was a shed with a pit dug into the ground. This was the storeroom or refrigeration room for the mess. It had a small trapdoor, which was locked at all times to protect its contents.

Beyond this, about fifty feet away, was another building one-third the size of ours, which, I found, was the residence of Sergeant Short, his wife, and the soldiers. Some one hundred yards west of our barracks were two more structures. They were constructed in a way similar to the barracks but were much larger, perhaps twenty feet in width by fifty feet in length. These were the two storage houses for potatoes. There were three other facilities in this complex with which I was to be intimately involved during my stay on the farm: rows of cold frames for seedlings, the stable, and the bathtub by the river. When I first noticed the stable, I said to myself, "Oh, so this is where *my* horses went," recalling the day they were removed from the camp along with the source of food for Yasunaga and myself.

Sergeant Short left us and walked toward his living quarters. "All right, men, go put your things in the barracks, and come out here and line up," ordered Spineless. Without the Russian present, Spineless sounded more assertive. We deposited our belongings hurriedly and assembled once again in front of our barracks. Spineless ordered us to go to the potato warehouse. Once inside, he explained that we were to sort out the spuds and prepare for planting. "What! I thought we were going to sort out the potatoes for our lunch," exclaimed Slim. "You guys haven't had lunch yet?" asked Spineless. "No," replied Slim and Mustache in unison, "they told us back at the main camp that the truck was bringing out our ration beginning at noon today and we'd get our lunch here." "Let me go check with the mess," said Spineless, and he walked toward the exit of the warehouse, where there were six steps carved in the dirt leading to the outside. As instructed by Spineless, we began to sort out the rotten potatoes from the good ones. "Man, if we had a fire, we could bake some potatoes to eat," said Slim. "All this food around us, and we're still hungry," I agreed. Some of the men began to eat the potatoes raw. I, too, bit into one and thought it was pretty good. As hungry as we were, anything edible was good.

We continued our task in silence, which was broken only with an occasional, "Wonder what's happened to our lunch." "I know what's going to happen to our lunch," offered Mustache, as the afternoon wore on. He said, "I've heard about these shenanigans between some of the mess workers and the Russians. The rumor is that the mess workers take the food to the village and trade it for some favors with the Russian women. With very few young Russian men available in addition to the shortage of food, what a great bargaining position for the cooks!" Sex was unimportant to the prisoners, whose stomachs were perpetually empty, even though they were in the prime of life. The conversation did not go much further. When Spineless finally returned, it was only to inform us that we could stop work now and go back to the barracks. The day's work was done, and it was time for supper.

The first week went by as we sorted the potatoes and quartered them in preparation for planting. Even here on the farm there was the clanging of the iron bar that signaled the beginning and ending of each workday, but the atmosphere was much more relaxed as the men gathered outside the barracks for roll call. During our second week, the next truckload of men arrived. This doubled the workforce in preparation for planting.

Other activities carried on by the men who were on the farm on a permanent basis included planting seedlings, taking care of horses, and making two trips during the day to a nearby pine forest to fell timber. They brought the timber back to the compound on their return trip, using a four-wheeled cart without a bed.

During my second week, Spineless approached me and told me to go join the seedling planters. Being the only temporary farm worker in this group, I first felt very much like an outsider. As the youngest among them, however, I had little difficulty finding my place—taking orders and doing what was asked of me. Actually, the group consisted of three men besides me; the youngest man treated me not as a subordinate but as equal with himself and showed great enthusiasm in his work, which set the pattern for me to follow. He reminded me of Imai, with whom I had worked in my basic training days. This man—I'll call him Copper for his dark complexion—appeared to be genuinely enjoying his work, unlike Imai, whose every action was planned solely to make life easier for us as well as for himself. The two of us climbed down the cliff to the river, filled a five-gallon can with water, and carried it back up the path hanging the can between us on a six-foot pole. We emptied the can of water into a larger container and returned for another load. The two older men took this water in a smaller bucket to water the cabbage seedlings. After two or three trips to the river, Copper decided that we had enough water.

We then got down on our knees and pulled the weeds out from among the seedlings in the hotbed. The warm sun felt good on my back as I crouched to do this task. It was hard to distinguish between the plants and the weeds. Having overheard me tell Copper of my difficulty, one of the older men came over and, with great enthusiasm, began to explain to me how this could be done. The other task of this group was to take care of the horses, which was routine. Feeding and giving water to the horses and cleaning the manure from the dirt floor was all that was required. One of the older men did all this, and I was asked to assist him when he appeared to be getting behind in his work. As I became used to the work, I realized that there really wasn't enough work for the four of us. To confirm my assessment of the situation, the older men told us to pace our work so that we would have something to do throughout the day. They cautioned us to be alert and look particularly busy when Sergeant Short came around.

The weather became warmer, and soon the ice was completely gone from the riverbank. In its place, wild plants and flowers began to sprout and bloom. The countryside suddenly became a lush garden, green and full of life. The camp population had now swelled to nearly a hundred men. The seedlings were ready to be transplanted to the field. One day the two older men were put in charge of all the planting operations on the farm. They gave instructions for preparing to plant the fields with potatoes and cabbages.

Spineless once again approached me and told me that I was to be in charge of the horses and the stable, and I began my duties immediately. Copper went to work in the mess because of the increase in the number of men now on the farm. I was busy in my new work, feeding the horses, taking their temperature once a day at noon and recording it, and cleaning out the stable.

With the countryside turning so green with thriving plant life, I took the horses out into the field to graze them. I tied a long rope around the neck of each horse and tied the other end to a post or a peg I had pounded into the ground. As they were feeding, I walked among them, sometimes brushing them with a metal brush. Occasionally, I lay on my back and gazed up at the sky, utterly relaxed. Seeing all the green vegetation around me, I was reminded of the hymn I had learned as a youngster in Imperial Valley, "I walk through the garden alone while the dew is still on the roses. . . ." For a brief moment, it was as though I were not in Siberia, a prisoner not knowing when I would be going home. Then in the distance I would see the other prisoners working in the field. I was aware of the work most of the fellow prisoners were doing, and I felt very fortunate that I was assigned as a stable attendant. I thought about the time when I would finally return to Japan and wondered what it would be like to live and work there. Work then certainly wouldn't be as easy as this. My thoughts wandered from one thing to another, but they always returned to going home. A horse neighed, and I was brought back to reality.

As the days wore on, it was soon impossible to take the horses out to graze at midday because of the terrible infestation of gnats. None of us had ever experienced anything like this in Japan. Swarms of gnats would appear from nowhere and viciously attack humans as well as livestock. The men working in the fields coated their faces, necks, and arms with oil and wore a net over their caps that covered their faces. They rolled down their shirtsleeves even in the warm sun. They did everything they could so as not to expose their skin to the insects. Many of them also lit a wick and attached it to their caps, which did help a little in smoking the gnats away. Even with these precautions, however, a number of men whose resistance was low were not able to cope with the situation and had to stop working when their faces got severely swollen and they developed a fever. During the worst time of the gnats' invasion, even the Russians who had lived on the farm all their lives were not completely immune to this plague and became bedridden.

During this period, I took the horses into the stable and made a mound of hay and dung on the floor and lit it so that the smoke would keep the gnats away. My eyes then became irritated and watery as I stayed with the horses in the smoke-filled stable. Staying indoors, however, I was not bitten by the gnats as badly as those whose work took them outdoors. One day a team of horses that had been taken to the forest by the tree men returned with blood streaming down their chests. Riding on the load of logs, the prisoners were not in a position to see the gnats on the chests of the horses pulling their load. I was in the stable and heard the team pull up outside. As usual, I went out to help them unhitch the horses and bring them into the stable to give them water and food while the cart was unloaded. Noticing the blood, I cried out for help. I got the men to help me put the horses in the stable immediately, washed the bloody area, and applied oil to it. Spineless was very agitated, but that was all we could do.

After this experience, I took special care to bring the horses into the stable during the worst part of the day and made sure the stable was well smoked.

Of the eight horses on the farm, one was a colt. It developed a fever one day, which I reported to Spineless. "There's an inspection visit by the Russians scheduled for tomorrow. We'll mention it to them at that time," said Spineless, who mumbled to himself, "I hope it's not anything serious." "I do, too," I agreed. "Huh, what?" said Spineless, with a look of surprise, as he turned around to face me. "I said that I agree. I, too, hope that the fever is not anything serious," I replied. A weak yes was his response, as I saw him scratching his head and holding his cap in the same hand. He continued, "The Russians really treasure these horses, and if anything happens to them, I'm responsible. They could make it hard on me." As I listened to him, I recalled how nervous Spineless became when the gnats ate into the skin of the horses. I remembered that he ordered me to place the two badly bitten horses in the corner stalls and do everything I could to keep them out of the Russians' sight.

As the colt's fever remained high even after the inspection visit, a Russian veterinarian was called to the farm. After checking the colt over, the veterinarian ordered it to be isolated. He left two handfuls of white pills with me and showed me how to wrap them in a moist piece of bread to give to the colt three times a day. The colt and I were moved down to the riverside next to the bath area, where I cleared a spot under a shady tree, and there I spent all my waking hours with the colt. A week later the vet came out to the farm again to see the colt. There was no improvement. Sergeant Short, Spineless, and a worker from the mess came with the vet, too. I learned that the vet had made the decision that the colt was to be destroyed. I left the place I had shared with the colt for the past week, making some feeble excuse that I would need to go up to the stable to help the man who had replaced me there. I climbed the steep riverbank up to the stable.

That afternoon the man from the mess, accompanied by a helper, skinned the colt and hung the carcass from a branch of the tree that had provided our shade. I was then called down and told to stay there to guard the meat. It was learned that whatever illness the colt had did not make the meat harmful for human consumption, and therefore it was to be taken back to the main camp as a supplement to the meat ration. A truck was arranged to come later that day to pick it up. It was getting late in the day, and I was about my work of filling the fifty-gallon drum that we used as a bathtub. I lit the fire under the can to heat the bathwater. This was part of my duty when I was transferred to take care of the stable full-time.

I sat under the tree late that afternoon, eyeing the meat hanging from one of the low branches and the fire burning under the can. I took out my knife and began cutting strips of meat. I threw them on the fire. I actually cooked and ate the very colt I had nursed for a week! Today I am able to say only that we prisoners were desperate men. Before the truck came around to pick up the meat, I took several more slices, which I wrapped in some large leaves off of plants growing nearby. I was very careful and removed strips from different parts of the carcass so that my actions would not be noticed. The men who came for it, however, were aware that I had taken the meat, but they only said jokingly, "Hey, there's pieces missing," and did not pursue the matter any further. I shared this meat with some of the workers who came around to take their baths later that evening. They all knew where the meat had come from but were grateful for the feast.

16. The Death of Yoshida: "Suicide of Two Lovers"

The death of Yoshida was one sad and ironic incident that marred my memories of the almost leisurely days on the farm. Yoshida, a man of slight build with a mole on the right side of his nose, had been in the Japanese Army two years before the surrender and was one of the three men assigned to the tree-felling group. The accident happened toward the latter days of my stay on the farm. The pine forest where the three men did their felling was located some distance from our barracks. To get there, the loggers traveled a country road that cut across other collective farms where the Russians worked. Although our own crop of potatoes was not yet ready for harvesting, some of the other fields had had an earlier start, and the potatoes were now large enough to be harvested.

On the fatal day, as the group was returning from their morning work of tree felling, Yoshida looked back, made sure that the Russian guard who went along with them could not see, jumped off the logs, and ran into the field to steal some potatoes. He wrapped what he had taken in his jacket. When they arrived at the compound, Yoshida was afraid of carrying his bulky jacket with the potatoes back to the barracks as the guard might become suspicious. On a usual day, the three would leave the load on the cart and join the other field-workers in the barracks for lunch. They would then ask for extra help after lunch to unload the timber. That particular day, Yoshida insisted that they

unload the timber before they went to eat because the Russian guard would, by the time they were finished, be gone for lunch. He volunteered to carry one end of the heavy timber himself while the other two were to carry the opposite end. The timber had been cut only that morning and therefore was wet and heavy. The three lifted the timber off the axle onto their shoulders. They were to throw it to the ground on the count of "three." The two cleared their heads from under the load. However, Yoshida's end was too heavy for him, and, not being able to duck at the proper moment, he fell to the ground with the timber on his shoulder. His head was crushed by the weight.

We were all sitting on our bunks, eating our noon meal, when the accident happened. One of Yoshida's companions came dashing into the building and yelled for the first-aid man, "Hurry! Hurry! Something terrible has happened! Yoshida's badly hurt!" We all stopped eating. No sooner had the two left than Yoshida's other companion ran into the barracks. "How's Yoshida?" asked Spineless. "No good," came the reply in a shaky voice. "This is Yoshida's bunk, isn't it?" He took out a clean pair of undergarments and went back out. It was an old Japanese custom to put something clean on a corpse before cremation or burial. Stunned by the instant death of our fellow prisoner, we were immobile and silent. During roll call that evening, Spineless lectured us on how careful we must be in our work. "We don't know when we will be able to go home," said Spineless, "but when Yoshida was killed this noon, Sergeant Short said, 'What a terrible thing to happen when it's so near the time when you people will all be going home.'"

Someone on the farm began referring to the accident as *shinju*. *Shinju* is a suicide involving more than one person, usually two lovers who, forbidden to be united for some societal or family reason, take their own lives with a prayer that they may be united in death. In this case, *shinju* was between Yoshida and his potatoes. Perhaps it was an unkind remark to make in the face of such a tragedy.

17. Locked in the Guardhouse

One evening Spineless announced that the Russian officers from the main camp would be arriving for inspection the following day. "This is going to be the real thing," he said. From the tone of his voice and his gesture, one could tell he was nervous. It reminded me of the military training period in my school days as well as in the army. The instructor and our superior would become nervous and tense before an inspection, in which they were to be graded by the performance of those under their command. "Everyone is to be out in the field tomorrow planting potatoes," he continued. "There will be only one left in the mess. Suzuki, you, too. No need to stay with the horses tomorrow."

Out in the field the following day, I was paired with Mustache. We worked as a planting team, with one of us taking a shovel to dig holes and the other following with a bucket filled with spuds. The bucket man would also cover the hole by pushing dirt with his shoes after dropping a spud into it. The field was laid out with rows made by a worker driving a horse pulling a plank twelve feet long with seven spikes in it. The field was not well smoothed out after the plowing, which left the surface with many large clods, and thus the marking made by the plank and spikes was difficult to see and follow. A team of planters took three rows, moving from left to right as they worked their way down the field. The shoveler walked backward, digging a hole every two feet in each row. I soon got the rhythm of the work and was enjoying it. Everyone was working hard, talking very little, when the inspecting officer finally arrived. It was early afternoon. The planters kept on, going up and down the field. The three markers were being pushed to their limits, it seemed, as they seldom paused to rest the horses. A team of two horses pulling a large four-wheeled wagon brought the potato seeds from the storage to the field. They were unloaded at one end of the field, where the planters returned to fill their buckets.

Once I was filling my bucket with potatoes just as the wagon arrived. I overheard some of the planters tell the wagon driver to persuade the loaders at the warehouse to make the load lighter since the work of the planters was usually determined by the number of wagon loads per day. "Can't do that today. They're watching them at that end, too, and making them load the wagon to capacity," the driver replied. "I can take care of that," said the worker standing by me, as he looked around the field to see where the Russians were. Finding them all at the opposite end of the field, he grabbed a shovel from another man and began digging a shallow hole. He emptied his bucket of potatoes into it, as others standing close by did the same. They covered the hole quickly. The first planter with the shovel dug another hole, which was soon filled with potatoes and covered. We all returned to the field and continued our work. Back at the field, I told Mustache about what had happened. Not at all surprised with my report, he said, "That's nothing new. We do that whenever we can. Gotta keep ahead of the Russians, you know." As I continued our work silently, I thought to myself, what will happen when the potatoes begin to sprout from those holes? I'd sure hate to be around then.

We continued digging, throwing in the potatoes, covering the hole, and repeating the steps over and over again. Suddenly I became aware of Sergeant Short following us. "What's he doing?" I asked Mustache. "Yesterday when I was planting," answered Mustache, "I couldn't hold on until noon, so I took off to relieve myself during work. My partner took my shovel and carried on, doing both the digging and the planting by himself, and, of course, he fell far behind by the time I returned. So, to catch up with the rest, I began spacing the holes farther apart. We caught up in no time, but then Sergeant Short followed us as we worked and gave us both hell for our sloppy work."

I suddenly realized that something was wrong the way we were planting and said, "Hey! Wait a minute. Aren't we doubling up? I think this first row on your left is really the last row of the group on your left! We're doubling up on that row and skipping our last row on the right." No sooner had I made this discovery than Sergeant Short began to curse loudly and summoned Spineless to the spot. "We're going to get it now," said Mustache, disgusted. Being told what had happened by the sergeant, Spineless yelled, "What's the matter with you guys?" He turned to the sergeant and said repeatedly, "No good work! No good work!" Presently, one of the Russian guards was on the scene. Sergeant Short said something to him, but all I could make out were his curses and the words, "Hurry up, hurry up." "Go with the soldier," Spineless rumbled. "You two really screwed it up." We dropped our shovel and bucket and returned to the barracks with the Russian soldier. What kind of punishment would we receive? We dreaded it.

"What are you doing back so early?" asked the kitchen man. As Mustache began to explain what had happened, the guard proceeded to say something to the kitchen man, pointing toward the food storage pit. I was only able to understand the words *cold* and *hurry up*. Our kitchen man told us to fetch our overcoats and put on all the warm clothing we possessed. As we came out of our barracks, the guard led us to the pit and opened the trapdoor. Although it was dark, I was able to see the wooden ladder leaning down the side. The guard suggested that we put on our overcoats and then motioned us to climb down the ladder. I went down first, with Mustache following. In the darkness, I felt sawdust under my boots. "Cold?" the guard asked. "Yes, c-o-l-d," we answered.

It was pitch dark at first. However, sunlight did come through the cracks in the trapdoor and, as our eyes became accustomed to the darkness, we were able to make out the objects in the pit. "Hey, look what's over here in this barrel," said Mustache excitedly. "There's milk in this barrel. It's about half full." "These boxes," I added, "must be fish. This one is open, and I think it's dried herring." "What luck! Good!" exclaimed Mustache. Everything was made to order. There was a dipper in the barrel, and we took turns drinking the milk. The fish was tasty, too, and, naturally, we ate and drank until we were full. We then arranged the boxes so that we could lie down on top of them. We bent our legs to lie down on our makeshift bed and soon fell asleep.

I was awakened by the sound of the trapdoor opening. I got up quickly and sat up on the box. There was no time to wake Mustache. The door opened, and I could see it was the guard. "Cold?" asked the guard. "Cold, very cold," I answered, hoping that the guard would not notice Mustache asleep. However, he, too, was awake now, and, still lying down, he said, "Very cold, very cold." He began to move toward the ladder pointing to himself and then pointing up. The guard, however, grabbed the wooden ladder, shook it, and said, "No, no. No good. No good work. Cold all right." The guard laughed loudly and closed the trapdoor over our heads again. Mustache took another drink of milk, and we both lay down. Before we knew it, we had both dozed off again.

We were awakened this time by Japanese voices above the trapdoor. The light coming down to the pit was very faint, and we knew that the day's work was over and that all the men had returned from the field. "Hey, you two." It was Spineless. "You can come out now." "Please open the door more. It's dark down here, and we can't see well," I answered. As we climbed out, Spineless couldn't wait to admonish us, saying, "I warned you about what an important day today was to be. Everyone was doing his best to show how well we work here on the farm. You two really made a blunder." We both stood before Spineless with our heads bowed and listened to him, doing our best to look remorseful and repentant. He had no idea how grateful we were to him for the rest from work in the field and the feast we had enjoyed in this food storage pit. Some punishment!

Word of what had happened must have gotten to the Russians. Later during our stay on the farm, the Russians made sure that all the accessible food was removed before anyone was imprisoned in the pit. Furthermore, they locked offenders up after the day's work was over, not during work hours.

18. Ground Squirrel Trapping: A Kind of Freedom

The cabbage and potato plants were growing as superbly as the wild plants in the countryside. It was as though they were racing against time to reach maturity before the cold season would set in again. Another prisoner was assigned to the stable to replace me when I was sent to stay with the sick colt. With the death of the colt and my job at the stable gone, I knew I would join the others to work in the fields. Then came the day I had long been waiting for. It was noon, and all the men had just finished their lunch in the barracks. Spineless walked over to the center of the barracks and stood there with his hands on his hips. Turning his head from left to right, he called out, "Are there any volunteers for catching squirrels?" Even before he completed his call, I jumped off the bunk and cried eagerly, "Yes, I'll do it!" "Oh, it's you, Suzuki," said Spineless. "Do you think you can do it?" "Yes, I'm absolutely sure I can. I heard all about what the work involves from the two who did it last year. They were from my neighboring squad back at the main camp," I replied, trying hard to sell myself and, at the same time, not to look too anxious. "OK, you can begin this afternoon," said Spineless. I had anticipated some competition in getting this assignment and was happy that no one else had come forward.

I washed my meal plate in a hurry and walked over to the Russian quarters together with Spineless. I was given half a dozen metal traps there. As soon as Sergeant Short began to explain how I was to use the traps, I indicated to Spineless that I knew all about how to use them as well as what I was expected to do with the fur. Sergeant Short smiled and said, "Good! Good! Catch a lot." With the traps in my hands, I went back toward our barracks. Spineless was standing by the door when I came out of the building with a pillowcase for me to put my catch in and carry it back. He stopped me and said, "There is no quota in your work. But catch as many as you can, and remember to turn in the pelts to Sergeant Short. That's all he wants." I then went around to the side of the kitchen hut and picked out six straight pieces of firewood to use as stakes. To these I secured the traps with wire. Now I was ready.

I left the compound together with the men who were leaving for the field. The men with hoes on their shoulders veered to the right and followed the road, while I went straight ahead and cut across the field and headed in the direction of the knoll. I soon came across the first squirrel hole, which brought back memories of my very young days in Imperial Valley, California, where I often accompanied the trapper who did the same thing I was now doing, trapping gophers that burrowed in the banks of the irrigation canal and caused floods. The only difference was that the squirrel holes I was to look for did not have the mound of dirt around them as those dug by the gophers did. I knelt at the first hole to set my trap. I tapped the stake into the ground, made sure that it would not move, and then got up and continued my zigzag trek through the field. I had no difficulty finding the nests. It became clear that six traps were not nearly enough, and I told myself to ask for more that evening on my return to the compound. Thus began my second stint at solo work, after my short time in the stable.

Crisscrossing the fields, and sometimes climbing the knoll, I thoroughly enjoyed my new "freedom." Later in the afternoon, as the sun began to go down, I took the bag with my first day's catch and climbed down the riverbank to the bathing area. I skinned the squirrels there, washed the meat in the cool river water, and nailed the pelts to odd-sized boards I had picked up around the compound. I took the meat and threw it on the fire burning under the drum can bathing tub. Together with the helper from the mess, who was tending the fire, I ate the squirrel meat. Soon the field-workers began to arrive, and they, too, shared in this feast. "Good show!" said Slim in a loud voice as he wiped the black smudge from around his mouth after devouring a squirrel by himself. I told him that I could easily catch many more if only I had more traps. I mentioned to him my plans to see Spineless about getting additional traps later on. He agreed that it was a good idea but also suggested that I should be able to come up with some kind of a homemade contraption, too.

Some of the men were standing around, waiting for their turn to get into the tub while listening to this conversation. They had not eaten the squirrel meat as they were not sure if it was wise to do so. They thought that the squirrels were carriers of malaria parasites and that, by eating it, we would contract this disease. I knew that the two men who had done this work last year came down with malaria after returning to the main camp, and it was widely rumored that the cause was the squirrel meat they had eaten on the farm. I remembered hearing from them that they took a chance knowing that this might happen simply because they were hungry, and, besides, they thought they could avoid going to work if they became ill. I thought about all this, but I, too, was hungry and felt that it would be worth the risk if I could, because of illness, get on a patient list to be sent home. Clearly, we were young and reckless and made our decisions without giving much thought to anything beyond our immediate needs.

I climbed up the cliff path with my traps and catch; I placed the boards with pelts on the fence adjacent to the stable where I thought the exposure to the sun would speed up the drying process. I went into the barracks and joined the other men for supper. That evening, as I lay on my bunk, nursing my legs, which were heavy and tired from all the walking through the fields, I mulled over my incredible good fortune in landing this trapping job. I was also pleased with the three additional traps that Spineless was able to acquire for me. Although they did not work properly, I knew I could repair them. As I pondered what Slim had said about making some sort of homemade trap, I drifted off to sleep.

Although the days were long, I enjoyed this new carefree environment. I did come up with a new trap, which was a very simple device. I used some heavy twine and made a small loop. I coated the twine with soap to make it stiff so that the loop would be even and form a perfect circle, then tied one end of the twine to a stake. To set this trap, I pounded the stake into the ground over the squirrel hole and positioned the stiffly coated loop in such a way that it was centered on the hole like a lasso. To my surprise and joy, this crude contraption worked! I caught more than three dozen squirrels on a good day.

One day I came on three large white objects among the potato plants. I first thought that they were dry, bleached bones of some animal. Looking more closely, I saw that there was a shine to them, but I still was not able to tell whether they were some kind of living creature or vegetation. I called over to the men walking along the road toward their afternoon work. One of them came over and identified them as Mongolian mushrooms. He assured me that they were edible and suggested that I pick them and take them back to eat. On my return to the compound that evening, I took one of the mushrooms to the kitchen. The cook was glad to receive it and said that if I needed something I should let him know. I did not ask for anything at the time; later, however, I received some extra rations from him when I moved on to my next job as watchman. Sergeant Short seemed to be satisfied with the quantity of pelts I turned in to him, as he always said, *Kharasho, kharasho! Spasiba!* (Good, good! Thank you!). The hidden primary purpose of my squirrel-catching job was, of course, for Sergeant Short to have the pelts (it was said that he sold them to earn extra cash). As Spineless had explained to me at the beginning, catching the squirrels did not really help alleviate the damage to the crops done by the animals, but I most certainly benefited from and enjoyed the easy work.

19. Watching the Watchman

It was July, and the temperature kept rising. The cabbages began to form their heads. Sergeant Short came to Spineless one day and told him that it was time to station two men as guards in the field to protect the vegetables from hungry Russian thieves. This was a twenty-four-hour duty to be handled by two men. I was assigned as one of the two and was joined by Hashimoto, a man in his mid-thirties. I learned later that he had been a farmer in Japan and that he received his pink paper (draft card) and was called back to active duty in early 1945. Hashimoto was shorter than I and had a triangular face, with a very large nose for a Japanese.

I had some misgivings about this setup of working as part of a close-knit team mainly because of my difficulty with group living. I thought about the discomfort I felt in the barracks situation at the main camp, where we slept, ate, and worked in such close proximity and without any private space. I was afraid that being isolated with Big Nose in cramped, makeshift quarters would prove even more challenging for me. I soon found that all my anxiety was needless. Big Nose was not bossy. He was helpful but not patronizing. There was only one thing he insisted on. Big Nose said that all the food preparation should be left up to him. This was exactly what I wanted! I couldn't have asked for more. My "cooking" was limited to throwing the meat on the

open fire or throwing the potatoes in the embers. No, Big Nose said that I must leave the cooking to him. What luck!

The first day at this job we began the work of constructing a shelter for ourselves. It was left up to us to determine where this was to be. We picked out a place near the road that cut through the middle of our field, about half a mile from the compound. We dug a hole four feet by seven feet and four feet deep. We covered the pit with birch limbs to form a ridge and thatched these branches with smaller birch branches and hay from the stable. We also laid some hay on the dirt floor and put down a straw mattress from Big Nose's bunk. The pitched roof was built so that it was just high enough for us to stand when we were inside. It was large enough for just one of us to sleep in while the other was on duty. There were steps cut into the dirt at one end for us to climb in and out. At this same end, we added a flat shed five feet square, supported with a larger branch at the four corners. It was a little more than five feet high so that we could stand underneath without hitting our heads. It took nearly two full days for the two of us to complete this project. As Big Nose threw the last twig on the shed, we both stood back to admire our creation. "Wait a second," said Big Nose. "We need to put the little paper strips on the roof for the topping-off ceremony." With the addition of the traditional Japanese paper strips, our project was now truly finished.

After congratulating ourselves on the fine work we had done, we sat beneath our front shed to discuss our duty. There really wasn't much to say, except that we would take turns on watch. We were stationed here to guard our potato field against any theft by the Russian villagers. As it turned out, neither Big Nose nor I ever encountered anyone attempting to steal from our farm during our stay there. If anyone did, we were not aware of it. Big Nose did all the cooking, as was agreed on. We also continued to catch squirrels, which was primarily my job. We returned to the compound to pick up our food ration every three days or so.

Our work soon fell into a routine pattern, although there were some different experiences along the way. One evening, as Big Nose was cooking our supper, he began to sing in his raspy voice, "Just ol' prisoners, catching squirrels. Not a Russian in our world. . . ." The song expressed our joy at being away from everything and everybody, especially Russian guards. "Hey! What's this?" I asked, noticing the potatoes Big Nose was peeling to add to the pot, which already had some squirrel meat and oats in it. "That squirrel over there," answered Big Nose, pointing to one hanging from the shed roof, "he led me to these, ha ha. I chased him into his hole, and when I began digging after him to set the trap, I came across these potatoes. You know, I think the Russians have a better variety than we do, and theirs are all ready to harvest." "Come on, you wouldn't be trapping squirrels in the Russians' field," I chided him, knowing full well that he went in their field only for the purpose of raiding their crop. "You'd better watch out," I cautioned. "They have a watchman on their field, too, you know." "Yeah," he replied, "but he's an old man. He'll never catch me taking his potatoes. The only thing I should be careful about is to bury these peelings so our guard doesn't see them when he comes around." I picked up the peelings and buried them in a shallow hole behind our shelter.

Early one morning, when Big Nose was on night duty, he planned to leave the shed before daybreak, go to the Russian farm, and bring back vegetables, such as carrots and onions, that he knew they grew there. Despite this plan, he fell asleep on duty, and when he woke up, it was nearly dawn. Although he knew he was getting a late start, he grabbed our pillowcase bag and dashed off toward the Russian farm about half a mile away in the opposite direction from our camp compound. He arrived at the Russian farm and went into the carrot patch, making sure that the coast was clear, and began digging. Big Nose was careful in digging the carrots so that it would be difficult to notice that any had been dug. He had to space carefully and cover the ground after he dug the carrots. Next came the onion patch. Here again, he took extra care to remove the plants so that it could not be detected.

Big Nose was so absorbed in his raid that he was not aware of the Russian watchman at the other end of the field. When he finally saw the watchman, Big Nose fell down on his stomach and lay still. Fortunately, the watchman did not come toward him but walked back and forth at the opposite end of the field. Big Nose lay still for a while and then raised his head to take another look. It was getting lighter rapidly, and he knew that he had to get out of the Russian field. He crawled for some two hundred yards to where the field bordered a wooded area of lanky birch trees. It was in the vicinity of where we had gathered some of the material to make our shelter. Crawling into the woods, he finally felt safe, got up on his feet, and began to trot back.

It was daybreak, and I began to wonder what had happened to him when he finally returned to our shelter. It was a great relief for me to see him safely back, and, from the bag he carried in his right hand, I knew what he had been up to. "What happened?" I asked as soon as he was within talking distance. "That was a close call," said Big Nose with a sigh of relief. "I was really lucky. The watchman was guarding the field, but he kept walking at only one end of the field, and I was able to crawl to safety. . . . Midnight raids only from now on." We both relished the soup that Big Nose made that morning, knowing the onions and carrots in it were acquired at such great risk.

The days wore on. I felt that the nights were getting cooler, and it was good to sit by the fire after supper. Smoking our tobacco, we watched the sunset turning the western skies into a beautiful brocade of orange and gold hues. We heard the clanging of the evening roll call bell drifting toward us from the compound. Big Nose began to hum a favorite children's song about evening and going home:

> The sun is setting in the west; the evening glow lights the horizon, and the dusk is setting in. I hear the temple bell ringing from the hilltop. Let us all hold our hands together and go safely home.

"You notice the heavier layer of fat under the squirrels' skin these days?" asked Big Nose. It was a definite sign that summer was coming to an end. "I hear that there are some wild burdock plants growing by the river," he continued. "If you can dig some burdock plants tomorrow, I'll make some *kimpira-gobo*." (*Kimpira-gobo* is burdock root sautéed in oil.) True to his word, Big Nose whipped up a pan the next day of good old *kimpira-gobo* Japanese style, right there in the middle of Siberia!

One other vegetable was special. Eating the Mongolian mushroom was an experience, to be sure, but wild mushrooms began to appear very early in summer and continued to grow almost the entire time we stayed on the farm. During the height of the season, Big Nose and I would easily fill our pillowcase bag with them when we went into the birch woods. It would seem almost impossible to walk on the ground without stepping on them. We didn't need to pick them; we simply gathered as much as we wanted. There were many varieties, too. Some grew on the ground, while others grew on fallen branches and on trees. They came in various shapes and sizes, and in just as many colors. I was afraid to eat them at first, as I remembered reading in the newspaper in my younger days in California about people who died of mushroom poisoning. However, I was to learn quickly that one would know a poisonous variety by its bitterness or some other disagreeable taste. As I observed that most people were eating mushrooms without getting ill, I, too, began to enjoy them. As Big Nose and I had more mushrooms than we could possibly consume, we took many bagfuls to the camp kitchen, for which the cook rewarded us with an extra ration of fish or grain.

We also dried the mushrooms on the roof of our shelter. One day Sergeant Short and his wife came by on their horse-drawn cart and stopped by our shelter. She saw the mushrooms drying on the roof and asked what they were. Told by her husband what they were, she turned up her nose and said something to him. Although I did not understand her remark, her gesture and the look on her face led me to guess that she must have said something like, "What! Eat those dirty-looking smelly things? Poor prisoners!" Big Nose also observed the scene and said to me, "Listen to this know-nothing peasant. She wouldn't know a classy dish if she saw one." Big Nose rolled up his sleeves and cooked the mushrooms in a variety of ways. He sautéed them, made mushroom soup, and cooked them with rice or some other grain. As I watched him display his many culinary skills, I knew he was enjoying the appreciative attention of his audience of one.

It was the third week in August. As I climbed up the steps and stood under the front shed one morning, I saw light frost on the ground. It was enough to wither the leaves of the potato plants all around our shelter in the middle of the field. Summer was over. "It was cold last night," I said to Big Nose. "Yeah, even with the fire and my overcoat on, it got pretty cold sitting here," Big Nose agreed. The Russian guard came out at noon that day and told us to gather our belongings, return to the compound, and prepare to return to the main camp. My life of three and a half months on the farm would be over all too soon. I looked back over my shoulder and saw the shelter for the last time.

I could picture the shelter still standing after the first snowfall. With the first blizzard, it would be blown over. Next spring the snow would melt, and then summer would follow. Again some farmworkers, Russians, of course, would be sent to the farm since we would all be back in Japan by then. They would plant and harvest their crop. Our shelter would be all gone except for the hole in the ground. A squirrel would scurry around, stop, stand on its hind legs, and then dash into its hole to escape from something it saw in the distance.

We walked toward the camp in silence.

20. Destination: Coal Mines

The truck ride back to the main camp was not at all like the trip we took out to the farm back in May. At that time we had been enthusiastic and full of dreams of and hopes for the good life ahead of us. Needless to say, the anticipation of abundant food had been foremost in our minds (although it did not turn out exactly that way). Our future was uncertain now. We felt uneasy, particularly because of the way in which we left the farm. We were in the middle of harvesting the cabbage crop and had yet to begin digging the potatoes. It was sudden, to say the least, and we all felt something out of the ordinary was going to happen to us. Slim overheard Driver Sato tell Spineless that a group was being organized back at the main camp to be transferred to some other camp. An optimist in the group came up with the notion that we were to be sent back to Japan.

The truck left the bumpy dirt road and was traveling on a crudely surfaced street at a reduced speed. We were approaching the city of Krasnoyarsk. Presently, the whitewashed gates to the main camp came into view. The truck came to a halt in front of the gates, where two guards with the ever-present machine guns strapped to their shoulders stood together with an officer. Driver Sato leaned out of the window and called out, "I'm returning from the farm. Open the gates." As the guards unlatched the gates and pushed them open, Sato drove past the guards, saying, *Spasiba* (Thanks).

The truck stopped and parked in the open space just inside the gates in front of the low guardhouse. All of us in the truck bed stood up. The men from headquarters were standing around, Ohta among them. I waved at him as he, too, spotted me. We all climbed over the low sides of the truck bed and jumped to the ground. Ohta approached me, looked me over, and said, "You've got a good tan. You've put on some weight, too. That's good!" I nodded and thanked him for sending me to the farm. Ohta's superior from headquarters ordered us to line up so that he could check his list against us. We were then told to go over to the other end of the open space, where there were more prisoners standing around and waiting. The main gates that we had just driven through swung open again for another work group to come through. "That's Work Group 12," I heard someone say.

The new men joined us presently, and everyone seemed to be talking at once. There was animated conversation between those of us who had just returned from the farm and those who had remained at the camp. We all had some catching up to do about the situation of the camp for the past three and a half months. Our talk, however, quickly turned to the subject of what was going to happen to us. I looked around to see where Ohta was and found him with those from headquarters and three Russian officers. The Japanese camp leader turned around and called for our attention. He began, "This camp has been ordered to assemble two hundred men to be shipped out tomorrow morning. You are the majority of the two hundred they need. There are a few others from the kitchen and also from the dispensary who will join you. I would have liked all of us to leave this camp together and return to Japan. However, things are beyond my control. I don't know where you are going. I hope that you will all find the work at your new place not too harsh. I pray for your health and hope, as you all do, that the day is not too far off when we will be returned to our country."

Ohta began passing out sheets of paper with the names of the men to each group leader. Those of us who had come back from the farm were divided into two groups. There was much commotion, but by dusk the groups were sufficiently organized. We were all to return to our barracks and squads for the night. We would gather at this location in the morning with all our belongings and march to the railroad tracks to board the train.

I entered the barracks that I had left three and a half months before and found its physical condition pretty much the same. Yasunaga commented on my tan and weight as Ohta had earlier in the day. I immediately noticed that Bully was not around and inquired about him. I was told that his health had deteriorated so badly that he was finally transferred to the malnutrition unit. It was pity more than anything else that I felt for him, in spite of all he did to make my life miserable during those earlier days.

The next morning, I awoke to the familiar, still dreaded, sound of the clanging iron bar. I ate my last meal with my squad. There was hardly any time for us to exchange good-byes or "see you in Japan." A few men were already in the open space when I got there, and in no time the two hundred men were all assembled. Ohta came over to me and said, "Looks as though my sending you to the farm got you into this group. I hope the new work will be easy wherever you go. Please take care." He was visibly concerned about my future. He had always watched over me and used his good offices and position to put me in the easiest and best situation possible. I thanked him for all he had done, although I knew my words could not possibly express the depth of the gratitude I felt toward him. How was I to know then that this was to be the last time I would see him? We were counted before being taken toward the main gate. Five abreast, we walked out the gates of Camp 5 for the last time.

At the spur tracks, we again boarded the freight cars. The cars looked familiar, with wide planks dividing the two ends into upper and lower sections and the large sliding doors in the center of the cars. Apprehension mounted when the train came to the main tracks, as we tried to guess which way it would go, farther west or return east. Our halfhearted interest and curiosity, however, were not comparable to the high level of anticipation we felt aboard the train back in Manchuria two years ago. Once again the train turned west. "Maybe they're taking us to visit Moscow to participate in their celebration of the Five-Year Plan," someone said jokingly.

We arrived at our destination in the afternoon of our third day on the train. We slid open the side doors to our car. As I looked out, the sight of coal mounds as high as a four-story building met my eyes. So we've finally come to the coal mines, I said to myself. I knew the same thought went through the minds of the others. No one said much. Coal mines and prisoners. Somehow, that seemed to be the ultimate combination of hardship and suffering for anyone in captivity in Siberia.

Presently, the order came for us to get off the train. We picked up our belongings, jumped off the train, and walked in the direction of the front of the train, dragging our feet. From there the column moved along the tracks until it came to a wider road. We turned right onto the road. There was another mound of coal on our left. A truck passed by and raised a heavy cloud of dust around us.

I then saw three figures approaching us from the opposite direction. As they drew nearer, I saw that they were wearing miners' outfits, blue coveralls with buttons down the front. Their boots had black rubber on the foot portion and canvas on the upper half. The boots were short and reached only halfway to their knees. The men wore hardhats, and each had a lantern fixed above the beak. There were cables that ran from the lamps to the batteries strapped to their belts. Their faces were black with coal dust and soot. I could not have guessed that they were Japanese were it not for their height. I wondered if these men had previous experience in coal mines in Japan or if the Russians were putting everyone underground. All this was not a pleasant sight and reinforced the fear that had welled up within us as we looked out the train door only a short time ago.

We continued to walk in silence; each of us was in deep

thought, wondering what might be in store for us at this new place. The column came to a halt in front of a large whitewashed gate. On both sides of the gate, a high fence capped with barbed wire continued on. There was an arch above the gate to our new camp, unlike the gate back at Krasnoyarsk's Camp 5. What was more significant was the message on the arch, which set the tone for life at this camp. COMRADES! UNITE, AND WORK FOR THE PEOPLE! read the message, written in large, bold letters. Along the top edge of the arch, small red pennants waved in the breeze. Someone muttered a joke about the message that greeted us, but the Japanese guard who stood at the gate made it clear that this was no joking matter, that it was all dead serious. I noticed that there were no Russian guards or officers in sight except for the guards that escorted us from the train. That's good, I thought.

As we walked through the gate, the first thing that we noticed about the camp was its massive size and clean appearance. The wide path inside the gates was bordered with whitewashed stones, and the barracks resembled the ones to which we had become so accustomed in Krasnoyarsk. In addition, there were a bathhouse and a dining hall, which was a large building built high off the ground so that one climbed six wide steps to reach its entrance. "Go straight ahead toward the bathhouse with the tall chimney, and before you get there turn right. That's your barracks," said the Japanese guard. We passed through the familiar double door to enter our barracks. The same rows of two-tiered bunks greeted us, and we were quickly assigned to our bunks.

In the evening, a man from headquarters explained the operation of this camp. He first described how the work hours were set up at this camp. "Coal mines are operated twenty-four hours a day," he began. "Therefore, unlike the factory where you came from, we do not have a day when the entire camp is off work. Each worker will get a day off each week, but the group he belongs to will be working seven days a week. Depending on the size of your group, the number of men who are off will vary. Also, everyone must work on various shifts. This is done by rotating the shifts every two weeks. Most of you, I think, will begin on a day shift that is from 8:00 A.M. to 4:00 P.M. After two weeks of day shift, though, the group will move to the graveyard shift. That will be from midnight to 8:00 A.M. Two weeks later, the group will change to the swing shift, which runs from 4:00 P.M. to midnight. As you can see, each shift is eight hours long. The work is hard, and it is steady. I understand that most work at the factory halted in winter when the temperature dropped to -40°F or below. That will not happen here. When you actually go into the pits, you'll understand, but work must go on twenty-four hours a day, seven days a week, every week and every month."

He paused for a moment as if he were anticipating some comments or questions, but there were none. He then continued, "There are different tasks in the mines. I hope that your leader, together with your Russian foreman, will be able to assign the best position for each man." After describing a few of the dangerous aspects of work in the coal mines, he went on to explain the general operation of the camp itself.

"You will not have to wash dishes or prepare meals at this camp," he began. "That tall building that you can see out the window behind me, that is the dining hall. You will receive four tickets each day. There is one each for breakfast, lunch, and supper. The other one is for your bread ration for the day. It should be the amount you were receiving at Krasnoyarsk. The first ticket you will get will be marked *supper*, which you will use for supper tonight. When you go in, you'll see the window and know where to go—no need to explain the setup of the hall. After you eat your supper, you are required to turn in your plate or dish, and you'll be given a ticket marked with whatever the next meal is to be. Tomorrow morning, take your breakfast ticket to the window, and so on.

"Now you are probably wondering when you can eat on the swing or graveyard shift. That has all been arranged. The hall is open almost twenty-four hours a day. Remember, I said 'almost.' There is a schedule posted at the entrance, so I suggest that you read it and become acquainted with the times. I mentioned that the work here is hard. It is, and I think that all in all everyone does his best to do his share of work. Because of this, the quantity and quality of food is quite adequate here. I expect each of you to work hard."

He also mentioned the bathhouse and how it was open practically twenty-four hours a day, too, shut down only for a brief time each day for cleanup. There was a barber shop adjacent to the bathhouse, and everyone was expected to visit it regularly. He added quickly, before anyone could ask, "By the way, only certain officers and headquarters personnel are allowed to have long hair." ("Long hair" was hair long enough to comb.) "All of you will be required to have your hair cut short, the way you had it in service." His hair was long. He turned around to say something to his assistant, who then got up to distribute the meal tickets. I turned the ticket over in my hand to study it. It gave me an odd sense of security, for I knew at that moment that at least my next meal was assured.

I went out of the barracks after a while and walked over to the dining hall. It was a huge building in which there were rows and rows of wooden tables, three feet wide and six feet long, and benches on each side, all neatly arranged. As I walked in, three men in white garb were mopping the floor. It was 8:00 P.M., and the big evening rush was just over. The men mopping the floor were also members of the kitchen staff, I was told. I walked up to the window and handed over my ticket to receive my meal. I carried the plate to an empty table and sat down. Despite the remark the man on the headquarters staff had made about the quantity of food earlier, I was not impressed with what I saw in front of me that evening. The meal consisted of some kind of grain cooked with vegetables in a bland sort of way, which I ate without much interest. On returning my plate, I was given my breakfast ticket, with which I walked out the door, climbing down the steps to follow the path toward the barracks.

It had been a long day. I recalled the eerie feeling I had when, for the first time, I saw the coal mounds, the black faces of the mine workers, the slogan above the gate that glared down on us, and the inside of this new camp. My life was changing, and I was sure I'd be affected by the experiences in the months to come. This was the Kuzbas Coal Mines in Siberia. I closed my eyes and fell asleep.

21. Occupation: Coal Miner

There was no clanging of the iron bar at this camp. An announcer was sent out from headquarters to notify each barracks that it was assembly time for each shift. Because of the varying distance of the three mines from camp, however, the announcer came around three different times at each shift. The majority of us from Krasnoyarsk were to work at Mine 1, which was located approximately a mile away from camp. On the first day of work we were ordered to leave a little earlier than we would normally since we would be issued our coveralls, boots, and hardhats before we entered the mines.

There was much activity as we arrived at Mine 1. Men and women were jostling about in every direction. I later observed that this was a typical scene around the mines at shift time because there were twice as many workers, some completing their shift and others starting theirs. We were then taken to the large miners' hall. Within this structure was located a restaurant, a bathhouse, and the tool shop. We met our Russian foreman, a heavyset man with a round face and a small red pug nose. He had a toothpick in his mouth and wore a felt cap that appeared to be at least two sizes too small for his head. I could not tell whether he needed a shave or a bath—perhaps both. What was more important was that he was a jolly fellow and greeted our leader with a friendly slap on the back. In a high-pitched voice, he said, "This way, this way," and motioned to us to follow him. He took us to the tool shop, where we received our clothing, a lamp, and a battery. We were also given shovels and picks.

We then followed Jolly to the entrance of the mine. A large roof structure covered the entrance, under which were two lines of rail tracks leading into the tunnel and a foot passage for walking down on one side. We followed Jolly down this passage. On our left was a railing separating us from the tracks; on our right was the wall. Overhead every ten or twelve feet a naked bulb was burning, hanging from two electrical wires that continued down into the mine. As I walked down the narrow passage of the mine, with my body scraping the rocky wall, I couldn't put the frightening thought of a possible cave-in out of my mind. We soon arrived at a broad open space. Jolly motioned us to stand on one side of the tracks running down the middle. A trolley train came and stopped. Miners were getting off. I saw them all walking toward the direction from which we had just come. Having finished their shift, they were returning to the miners' hall. As we boarded the trolley, our Japanese leader told us to be careful and be sure no part of our body or any tools were outside the car. As soon as the trolley began to roll, I realized why his warning was so important. The tunnel became extremely narrow, and we were closed in by the walls, with very little room to spare. Although it was quite warm outside, the air was slightly damp, pleasant, and cool inside. In what seemed about ten minutes, the trolley stopped. Getting out, we fell into single file after Jolly and followed him.

We left the tunnel with the two pairs of tracks and entered a much narrower one. We stood outside our shaft. Protruding out of the shaft was the end of the conveyer trough, about five feet above the floor of the tunnel. We stooped down and squeezed our way under the trough to enter the shaft. There were twelve of us, including Jolly and the Japanese leader, to do the digging in this shaft. In addition, there were three Russian conveyer operators who had arrived before us and were oiling the machine and doing other maintenance work, such as clearing some of the coal that gathered around their machine. The Japanese leader explained to us briefly what our work entailed. "I have positioned you out along the trough with about five feet of space between each of you," he said. "Now what you must do is take your pick and shovel and dig that area of coal and throw it into the trough as it begins to move. The coal you throw in the trough will move down toward the lower end of the shaft where we came through and drop at the end of the trough into the hand trolleys parked underneath. There, a crew of trolley pushers will move the coal out to the electric trolley tracks, which will then carry it up to the surface. Remember, you are responsible for that five feet of coal in front of you. That is your quota for the day. Also, be careful while you dig. Watch for falling coal."

The conveyer operators started up the machine, and the trough began to move. I took my pick and shovel and began to dig. I soon learned that it was easier to remove the coal from the bottom so that the coal above would crumble off the wall. I then scooped up the coal and threw it over into the moving trough. We rarely paused or stopped to talk. As I looked up and down the line, I saw the headlamps moving about in the dark shaft. My thoughts drifted back to my village in Japan, where fireflies flickered here and there in the quiet summer evenings. There was, however, little time to dream of such scenes, and I was quickly brought back to reality by the thumping, pounding, and banging sound of the coal landing on the metal trough. I went back to my digging. I gradually became accustomed to the work, and, before long, the thought of cave-ins no longer entered my mind.

It was the fifth day of our work at Mine 1. Just as we arrived, I saw coming out of the door at the other end of the miners' hall a group of men followed by two Russian guards. "I wonder who they are?" I said to our Japanese leader, who was standing beside me. "They're German prisoners of war," he explained. "I'm told there are quite a few of them here in the mines," he went on. "When you talk with the Russian civilians, you will notice that most of them are very bitter toward the Germans and treat them

in a way prisoners of war are known to be treated. When I talked
to a German prisoner briefly, he said he envied us since we could
look forward to returning to Japan, whereas he had given up all
hope of ever being repatriated to his own country." I was sad-
dened to hear about this hopeless situation. Jolly approached us
and motioned for us all to follow him. Our leader called out to
the group, "Let's go." I turned around and saw the German prisoners being led away by the guards as I followed my group into
the mines for another day's work.

Once inside the shaft, I did not think about anything other
than the area of coal in front of me that had to be removed in the
next eight hours. This particular day, however, the sight of the
German prisoners kept flashing back in my mind. On our way
back to our camp that afternoon, I mentioned this to the man
beside me. He, too, had heard about the Germans' gloomy
future. He had heard from a trolley pusher who was working in
the mines that a frail and older German prisoner approached him
meekly to ask him what time it was because he knew that the
Japanese did not hesitate to phone the mine office to ask for the
time of day during work hours. The trolley pusher gathered from
such behavior that the Germans would not go directly to the
Russians for information, for they did not wish to show any sign
of weakness to the Russians. "They're proud people, those
Germans," said the man next to me. I later heard that they
adjusted their pace of work to the slowest or weakest to protect
them, rather than trying to keep up with the strongest, as their
Russian supervisor pushed them to do. This gave me hope that
when a group of human beings suffers together, their goodness
prevails and they help each other, if only to survive.

We were in our second week at Mine 1 when all the groups
were transferred abruptly to Mine 2, the mine we saw first when
we arrived here at the Kuzbas. Most of us were pleased with this
change as the mine was located only a few hundred yards from
our camp. We did not know of any great reason for this change.

Rumor had it that we were moved to the new mine so that we would not have any contact with the German prisoners.

My work changed at this new mine. I no longer went into the shaft but became a trolley pusher. In the first mine, I never got accustomed to the lamp on my head because of its weight. As a miner, I needed the headlamp so that I had light shining where I was digging; with this new job as trolley pusher, I clipped the lamp on my chest pocket, as did most of the others, so that the lamp dangled at a correct angle to focus at my feet, which helped me see the track ties as I walked behind the trolley toward the winch turntable.

Mine 2 was much smaller than Mine 1. Here we did not need to take the long trolley ride to get to the shaft where all the digging was done. The coal was not hauled out from the mines to the surface by train but brought to the winch turntable, where it was hooked onto a cable by two men and pulled up to the surface. The Japanese prisoners were in charge of most of the operations in this mine. The operators of the conveyer trough were also Japanese. We did have a Russian foreman, however. Unlike Jolly at Mine 1, our new foreman was tall and thin and wore his jacket completely unbuttoned, with both his hands tucked into its pockets and his shoulder stooped. In sharp contrast to Jolly, this man seemed to be always grumpy. He would say, *Bystryey, bystryey!* (Hurry up, hurry up!), spitting constantly. We would talk back to him, saying, "First things first," in Japanese, of course. He sounded as though he wanted us to enter the mines before we had our equipment ready or begin pushing the trolley even before the coal was in. We soon became accustomed to all his *Bystryey, bystryey!* and ignored him, which did not seem to anger him particularly.

I quickly got the hang of my new work. I was paired up with Hagi, who was my age and very energetic. Six pushers worked in three teams. We stationed ourselves at the front of the entrance to the shaft where the trough ended, and, as the trolley carts were filled with coal, a team of pushers pushed it toward the winch turntable. There was a slight incline to the tracks, which made it quite easy to push the load. However, there were bumps and small twists in the tracks, and, therefore, it was important for us to make sure that the loaded trolley be kept on the tracks. We had a hard time handling the trolley when it fell off the tracks because of its weight. It was crucial that we get the derailed trolley back on the tracks just as quickly as possible because of all the following loaded trolleys backing up behind. When faced with such a difficulty, we called for help from the other team members, and, with a piece of two-by-four for leverage, we went to work. The return trip in the opposite direction had a little climb, but the trolleys were now empty, and, with two of us pushing them, it was not heavy work. In fact, we became so efficient that we needed to pace ourselves as we made our round trip along the tracks underground in order to avoid having the six of us bunched up where the trollies were loaded. We did not want our efficiency to cause a decrease in the number of workers.

A very wet mine, Mine 2 had many places where the water was not only running down the walls but coming down from the ceiling like a shower. This must have been why the coal produced in Mine 2 was damp and seemed to create relatively little dust. Taking advantage of this wet condition, the men began to smoke in the mines. Smoking in the mines was, as anyone can guess, considered extremely dangerous and was strictly forbidden. We were often searched when we entered the mine to see if anyone had a flint light or tobacco on them. They also inspected our batteries as we turned them in at the end of the shift for the same reason. Each battery was sealed when it was issued to us, and the inspector made sure that it was returned sealed. This procedure was carried out thoroughly and strictly at Mine 1, but at Mine 2 we found things to be somewhat relaxed.

As Hagi and I were outside the shaft waiting for our next trolley to fill, the smell of dynamite fumes came drifting toward us. Russian miners did the blasting work in the mines to enlarge the tunnel where our trolley tracks ran. Smelling the fumes that would cover up the tobacco smoke odor, Hagi loosened his belt and slipped the battery to the front where he could reach it. He took a piece of copper wire three inches long from his cap where he had hidden it, broke the seal on the battery case, and then connected the wire to create a short. Hagi put the end of his tobacco to the wire as it glowed. He took a deep puff, and the tobacco was lit. He passed it to me as he buckled his belt again. The tobacco tasted exceptionally good. I recalled my short stint in the Japanese Army, when Imai and others told me how good tobacco tasted, especially when smoking was prohibited.

The team following us arrived at the trough, and our trolley was filled. We passed the tobacco to them, got behind our load, and began pushing it down the tracks, making our twelfth round trip of the day. Our eight-hour shift was over, and the diggers emerged from the shaft. We joined them, and, with the two men who operated the winch turntable, the group climbed up out of the mine.

22. Situation: Dangerous

Two accidents occurred during my stay at the coal mines.

The first involved a worker in the feeder tunnel that ran parallel to the trolley tunnel where I worked with Hagi and the other two teams. The feeder tunnel ran at the opposite end of the shaft, and, through it, the material to support the ceiling of the shaft, such as poles and other timber, was brought in. On this particular day, the workers in the feeder tunnel were having problems, and Hagi and I were asked to help them carry in the material. We were told that two men from their group were absent because of illness.

We arrived soon after the shift began and were given instructions on what to do. Our task was to carry in not only the usual material for supporting the ceiling but also some rails to extend the tracks. For some reason, a coal trolley was on the tracks in the feeder tunnel instead of the regular flatbed trolley to do the work. Hagi and I suggested that we use a flatbed trolley instead. The two regulars of the group, however, insisted that it was not necessary to remove the coal trolley from the line and that we should immediately load it with the rails, which we were to take to the end of the line. Because Hagi and I were not regulars at this job, we both felt that we should do as we had been told by the other two.

We loaded the rails on the coal trolley and began pushing it down the tracks. The load was top-heavy and felt as if it were going to tip over at every little bump. We were extra cautious as we pushed the trolley along. The tracks became smoother, and the trolley began to roll along at a faster clip. Hagi and I were in our familiar position of pushing the trolley from behind. The two regulars were guiding and supporting the trolley from each side. We seemed to be going down a slight incline, and the trolley picked up more speed. Before we realized it, we had come to the end of the line. The trolley with its load of rails left the tracks, swung to the right, and overturned, causing the rails to fall on the regular who was supporting the trolley on that side. The three of us frantically grabbed the rails to lift them off his body. He lay there motionless. One of the rails had hit his head as the load went over, killing him instantly. Blood was all over his face. He did not utter a sound. His hardhat must have flown off his head and was lying close by. Somehow, the light was not broken and was still burning. Ironically, he was the one who had argued most ardently with Hagi and me that it was unnecessary to change trolleys before we began our work. I should have argued with him a little more, I said to myself; this wouldn't have happened to him if he'd listened to Hagi and me.

We removed the rails and the trolley that fell on top of the man and laid his body on the flatbed trolley that his coworker had brought in. As we were pushing the body along the tracks, I noticed that the coverall worn by this dead prisoner was not worn out in places like my own. I asked the other two if either of them wanted to exchange his with the dead man's. "No, why don't you take it?" said Hagi, adding, "but there are some bloodstains on it, you know." "I've noticed that, but I think it's better than the one I have on," I replied. Once above ground, we carried the body to the bathhouse, where I made the exchange. I was surprised or even appalled at what I was doing. The struggle for survival had revealed itself again. Did I really think that this bloodstained suit was better than my old worn-out suit?

The next day, I went to work in my "new" coveralls, bloodstains and all.

The second accident occurred during the winter that year. The conveyer trough operators were required to enter the shaft before the diggers and others of the group so that they would have their machines oiled and ready for operation by the time the others took their positions. There were three operators in our group, and it was customary for them to rotate their positions at each shift. On this particular day, Yamada, an operator who had worked on the middle machine on the previous shift, was to move up to the top machine. He had entered the shaft before the others and had nearly completed his maintenance work on the middle machine when the other operators arrived. The one who was to take the middle machine that day told Yamada that he was to move to the top machine. Yamada refused to move, however, already having spent his time doing most of the maintenance work on the middle machine and insisted that he was at the right position. The second operator realized that further argument would be fruitless and agreed to move on up to the top machine himself to do his maintenance work. The conveyer trough machines were started on time, and the digging began.

The coal began to spew out from the trough into our trolley. The men inside the shaft wielded their shovels and picks to complete their quota. We pushed the loaded trolleys down the tracks, and the empty ones were returned to the front of the shaft, where they awaited their next load of coal. It was almost noon. Suddenly, the support poles around the middle machine gave way as the ceiling above began to crumble. It was unmistakably a cave-in. The diggers quickly headed in two directions, those farther up from the middle machine dashing toward the feeder shaft, while those below tumbled out of the shaft from the opening where the end of the trough came out into the trolley tunnel.

"What's up? What happened?" shouted Hagi. "It's a cave-in! Yamada has had it," cried one of the diggers. The foreman called the miners' hall, and the rescue team came into the tunnel immediately and climbed into the shaft. It was, however, too late to help Yamada. His body was crushed under tons of coal. When they dug his mangled body out, it was lifeless. Some diggers said that they heard his cry for help as the coal began to fall on him but that there was no way anyone could have helped him. According to one of the diggers, they could hear a grinding sound just before the coal began to crumble. The others agreed, however, that, if the machine was in operation, as it was at that time, it would have been impossible for Yamada to hear any such sound because he was next to the machine.

Yamada was a quiet, easygoing, and agreeable man, and I don't know to this day what made him so insistent on staying with the middle machine, the decision that cost him his life. It was his fate to be buried in the Siberian tundra along with the countless other prisoners who never realized their dreams of going home.

23. The Third Winter: Indoor versus Outdoor Work

Almost four months had elapsed since I arrived at this coal mine camp. It was late December, the third winter in Siberia. I remembered what the man from headquarters had said when we arrived at this camp. He told us that all work would go on no matter how cold it got. However, there was one consolation with this arrangement. As soon as we entered the mines and went underground, we found the temperature at a constant 65°F. Outside the mines, it was as cold as Krasnoyarsk, or perhaps even colder. Everything was frozen. A deep mist hung in the air as if it were frozen, and the smoke from the chimneys rose straight up into the gray sky. When I walked between the barracks and the dining hall or ventured outdoors for anything without protective covering, the dampness in my nostrils caused the inside of my nose to freeze, which was quite painful.

On one of those cold days, to my surprise I found Grumpy, our Russian foreman, walking along with us with a pick and shovel toward the entrance to the mine. It was unlikely that he was helping someone carry his tools into the mine. I was completely taken aback when I saw him in the shaft digging with the rest of the men when work began. "What's going on?" I asked Hagi. He had no idea what had happened either. We were too busy trying to make our quota that day to dwell on what was happening to our foreman. We learned later that his supervisor was in the shaft that day, watching over the work of the group in place of Grumpy.

During our graveyard shift a couple of weeks before this happened, there were three consecutive nights of extreme cold. As the trolley arrived above ground, the coal inside each trolley froze. When the trolleys were tipped over to be emptied of the coal, only a small portion of the load fell out, as the damp coal had frozen and a thick layer was caked to the inside of every trolley. As a result, each trolley was actually delivering only a little more than half its capacity of coal. On paper, the production of coal for our shift showed almost twice the actual amount, as the quantity was measured by the number of trolley carts that arrived at the top of the cable line. Since the men at the winch turntable were keeping tally of the number of trolleys they hooked to the cable, we all knew that our "production" far exceeded our average during those three nights. We prematurely celebrated our outstanding output record, but someone higher up on the echelon held Grumpy responsible for the discrepancy between the number of trolleys and the amount of coal and had him demoted. A curious thing happened to Grumpy with this demotion. His mood seemed to have changed completely, and he was no longer the grouchy foreman with a stooped back. When he emerged from the shower that afternoon, he walked among us smiling and slapping us on the back and said, "Work was good today! The trolleys were going around and around, and much was done!" Grumpy, no longer grumpy, continued to work with his pick and shovel with our crew.

Like the latrines in Krasnoyarsk, the facility at Stalinsk (now named Novokuznetsk) was an outhouse ten feet wide and forty feet long. There was an entrance at each end, which was simply an opening without a door. There was no provision for heating this structure. A center divider wall ran down the length of the facility. On each side of this divider was a low platform a foot high, with round holes cut out three feet apart, over which we squatted without touching the surface to relieve ourselves. We also stood there on the floor to urinate into the hole. The hole under the outhouse was dug ten feet deep. When winter arrived and everything froze, the excrement, too, froze in the shape of stalagmites. It was none too rare that some prisoners rushed to the toilet at night when it was hard to see anything in the dark and pulled down their trousers to squat, only to have their buttocks poked by the sharp point of the frozen excrement. It was not a laughing matter that they needed medical attention at the dispensary for this unfortunate injury.

On our day off, we were often required to do odd jobs around the camp. These tasks were referred to as "service work," which was a common practice in the Japanese Army. It did not take too much of our time, and our obligation did not go beyond two or three hours. Besides, unlike our days in the army, it wasn't just the younger men who were called out to take care of these odd jobs; everyone was assigned to the work quite evenly. Teams of four men were organized and worked in one-hour shifts. One of the tasks was to chip away at the stalagmites of excrement protruding from the toilet holes. We were given picks, shovels, and iron rods as tools. It was also necessary to chip the frozen urine from the platform and floor of the toilet. While performing this task, particles of "ice" flew up and got on our clothing. As long as we were outside doing the work, the particles were odorless. However, it was crucial that all the "ice" be brushed off our garments before entering a warm room during our break.

Once our team went into the warm barber shop for our break, where it was discovered that one of the men had not done an adequate job of brushing off the "ice" before entering the shop. As we were standing around the stove, the "ice" began to melt, which, as one can imagine, caused the room to smell like the toilet. One of the barbers looked over toward us and, twitching his nose, said, "What's that? Smells like somebody has some shit on him!" The guilty one shot back, "Don't tell me your shit doesn't smell! In fact, I'll bet guys like you who have all the easy jobs inside the camp are the ones filling up the toilets with all the stinky shit!" As the four of us left the barbershop to return to our work, the man who was accused of smelling up the shop looked at the rest of us with a smile and said, "I deliberately didn't brush off all the 'ice.' It was my intention to create that confrontation." This was one of the instances in which the men who labored outside in the camp did not hesitate to show their hostility toward those who worked indoors and had it easy.

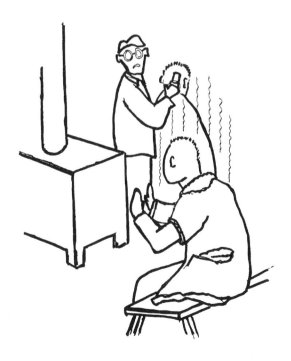

24. When English Became an Asset

It was my weekly day off from work. A visitor came into our barracks to look me up. He began, "Are you Suzuki-kun?" (*Kun* is a suffix used by men to address other men.) "I'm Yamamoto," he continued. "I'm also from Yamanashi Prefecture." Yamamoto sat down on the edge of my bunk and continued to talk about himself. He had graduated from Yokohama Technical College and was drafted into the army air corps, where he rose to the rank of captain and was shipped to the South Pacific theater. At the time of Japan's surrender, he was on a liaison mission to Manchuria and was captured by the Soviet Army along with the rest of the Japanese Kwantung Army, ending up at this coal mine camp with the original group of prisoners. I, too, introduced myself and told him of my past. We parted that afternoon and agreed to keep in touch.

On my next day off, Yamamoto the Pilot again paid me a visit, and this time he came with a large book under his arm. "Look at this, Suzuki-kun. A Russian novel, *Port Arthur*, and it's in English," he said. "I think it will be important for us to know English when we get back to Japan because it's the Americans who are the Occupation Forces there. I plan to use this book to study English, but you can keep it and read it, too. I hope you'll be able to help me brush up on my English." Pilot also handed me a small package, saying, "Here, take this—it's my bread ration for a couple of days. I can never get used to this heavy sour Russian bread." I was surprised that there would be a laboring

prisoner who couldn't eat Russian bread, or anything edible for that matter, when all of us, I thought, were perpetually hungry. As I was not sure if he really meant it, I declined his offer at first. I thought about my days in the army in Manchuria, where the officers and noncoms made it a practice to leave a portion of their meals on their plates for the hungry soldiers. I knew that quite a few Japanese soldiers could not eat the Russian bread in the early days of imprisonment. However, we had been here for quite some time now, and it was a surprise to me to find someone who still rejected it. As Pilot insisted that I take it, I finally thanked him and accepted the offer.

Pilot stayed on for a while and told me some more about his family in Japan. He then opened the book and said, "I've read through chapter 3. I'm struggling with the English but very fascinated with the novel. I have also glanced at some later portions of the book and find it very interesting. It's a new perspective on history, Suzuki-kun. What I'm finding here is the Russo-Japanese War from another point of view. The author, a Russian, of course, sees the historical relationship between the two countries quite differently from what we learned as Japanese. I feel we're going to run into plenty of new discoveries of this nature when we get back home. The invincible Japanese military has gone down in defeat! There must be a lot of changes back home." It was the first time that I had some inkling of what Japan's defeat meant for the entire nation. Up to that time, defeat was perceived only from the perspective of a soldier surrendering his arms, a company or a battalion put behind walls, and trainloads of soldiers shipped to Siberia. Now, Pilot brought a new dimension of Japan's defeat to my attention. We both sat in silence. The entry doors swung open as the men came into the barracks, returning from their day's work in the mines. We again agreed to meet on our days off as Pilot got up and left.

It was soon after meeting Pilot that I was visited by a prisoner named Iwata, who, like me, was a transfer from Krasnoyarsk. At Camp 5, Iwata had been a medic working in the dispensary during my stay there as a malnutrition patient. We were of the same age, and, having the common background of having lived in Tokyo, we had always considered ourselves friends in a casual sort of way. From early on, however, Medic Iwata tried hard to keep some distance between us for fear that his superior might accuse him of giving special favors to his friends. This being the situation, I was pleasantly surprised when he came by my barracks that evening. "How are you, Suzuki? I know that the work is hard in the mines, but you appear to be healthy. I have been fortunate. It was never guaranteed that I would land a job in the dispensary here, but here I am. I'm kept busy, but as you know, compared to the outside work, the work in the dispensary is definitely better," he said.

I asked if he had heard any news from Krasnoyarsk. Medic replied that he had had no contact with nor had known of anyone who had any news from Camp 5. I began to wonder what brought Medic out to see me. He looked as though he were leaving without telling me the purpose of his visit. As he picked up his boots, he motioned with his head for me to follow him. I got the message and stood up, reaching under the bunk for my boots as I said in a voice loud enough for those around me to hear, "I've got to go to the latrine. I'm glad you came over this evening. I hope the next time you come, you'll bring some good news about our return to Japan."

We both walked toward the entrance door. As we stooped over to tie our laces, Medic whispered, "There's a guy I've met at headquarters who would like to meet you. His name is Kako, and he's in charge of personnel here at this camp. I think it would be good if you go see him at your earliest opportunity, maybe tomorrow, as soon as you return from work. Tell him that we met and you got the message." I thanked Medic as he turned and walked toward the dispensary building. I stood there a moment and wondered what was in store for me in this new turn of events. The frozen snow creaked under my boots as I walked toward the latrine building.

After finishing my evening meal at the hall the following day, I went directly to the headquarters building. I found Kako at his desk working with a large ledger opened in front of him. "Exactly like my good friend, Ohta," I thought to myself. "Are you Kako-san?" I began. "I'm Suzuki. Medic said you wished to see me." "Yes, yes," Kako replied. He looked young, friendly, and enthusiastic. He said, "I have an English-Russian dictionary here. I know very little English, in fact, only what I learned in high school, and I have just as little Russian. I know it's a big project, but I wonder if you'd be able to start working on a Japanese-Russian dictionary using this. I can arrange to have you come here to do the work. What do you think? Would you like to give it a try?" "Yes, I would like to do it very much," I responded. "It sounds like a big task, but I can see a big benefit in it for me, too! After all the time I have spent here, I know very little Russian, almost none really. When will I start?" I asked eagerly. "Very soon," said Kako, "within a week after I can complete the arrangements. In the meantime, take this dictionary with you. I'm glad you will do this for me."

Dictionary in hand, I left the headquarters and returned to my barracks. I went to my bunk, and, before putting the dictionary inside my bag, I flipped through its pages once more. "My gosh! Translate an entire dictionary," I gasped. The realization of the enormous task finally began to sink in. Compared to the physical labor of working in the mines, however, it was easy to see which would be the choice.

25. Malaria

A few days after my visit with Kako at headquarters, I woke up early, even before the 6:00 A.M. reveille, feeling feverish and dizzy. With the arrival of the announcer, the barracks came to life. I walked over to the group leader and told him of my fever. He put his hand to my forehead and confirmed, "Yeah, you do have a fever. Go over to the dispensary before breakfast and see if the doctor can give you a diagnosis and an emergency release from work today." I walked along the frozen path to the dispensary. The doctor was not in, but a first-aid man advised me to go to work with my group and, as soon as I arrived at the mines, to obtain my Russian foreman's permission to go to the first-aid station there. He felt my forehead and added that I would surely be sent back to camp. He further explained that, without the Russian doctors' presence at the dispensary, the Japanese doctors did not have the authority to give me a release from work anyway.

I thought of the Japanese doctor at Krasnoyarsk who insisted on keeping those he diagnosed as ill from going to work. While I was there under his care I often heard him argue with the Russian doctors about the condition of his patients. I learned quickly that the situation here was quite different. Both Japanese doctors here were spineless "yes men," just as Numato had been on the farm, making no effort to stand up for their patients' rights. As the sick and injured came into their office to be diagnosed, they went through the motions of examining them with their stethoscope and hands. Then they waited for the Russian doctors to do the same and let them make the decision. I heard that even when they knew that a worker was ill and therefore needed rest, they did nothing to help him lest they displease the Russians.

I was also told that in the earlier days, the Japanese realized that the easiest way to become a patient was to have a fever. Some of the prisoners would warm a stone on the *pechika* in their barracks, wrap the stone in a piece of cloth, and put it in their armpit. When they were given a thermometer in the doctor's office, they inserted it in the warm armpit, which naturally registered a "fever." It was not too long before the Russians caught on to this trick, and, as a result, every patient was required to stand with his shirt off and his arms held up over his head for a length of time before he was examined. I was reminded of all the cat-and-mouse games we had played with the Russians in our foundry work at Krasnoyarsk.

Back in my barracks, I sat on the edge of my bunk with my overcoat on, waiting for my group to return from the dining hall. The group leader walked over to me and asked how the visit to the dispensary went. I told him of the situation and that I was advised to go to work with the group and visit the first-aid station there. It was mid-February 1948. Although I felt quite ill, I trudged to the mine. On my arrival, the leader took me immediately to the foreman and told him of my condition. The Russian nurse at the first-aid station did not even bother to take my temperature. She felt my head and told me that I should return to the camp instantly.

I saw Medic in the camp dispensary. He recorded my condition and the circumstances from earlier that morning and said that I was to return to my barracks and stay there until the regular evening examination hour. Early that afternoon, my group returned from work and found me in my bunk. "Still have that fever?" asked the leader. "I heard that you were on the farm before coming here and that one of your duties was catching ground squirrels. Eating squirrel meat will give you malaria, you know," he said, looking quizzical. I nodded and replied, "Yes, I don't know how many squirrels I ate last summer, but this sure doesn't feel like malaria to me. I was told one would get the shivers along with a high fever."

I reported to the dispensary during the regular examination hour that evening. I was running the same fever of 104° and was given a permit slip to stay out from work the next day. The fever persisted, and another permit slip was issued the following day as well. As the fever did not subside even after the third visit, I was ordered into the dispensary ward. The fever was no longer constant; it came on around 2:00 P.M. every other day and was accompanied by violent shivers. It was now definite that I had contracted malaria, and the treatment began.

An aide came to my bed, put two yellow pills in my mouth, and gave me a glass of water to wash them down. As I took the pills the second time, I thought to myself, "What am I doing? If I take those pills, I'll be well and will have to go back to work. Furthermore, spring will be here soon, and that means they'll probably be organizing a repatriation group. If I'm a patient at the right time, I may be able to get on that list and get back to Japan!" With this thought in mind, I managed to maneuver the pills under my tongue and hold them there while I swallowed the water. I spit out the pills after the aide was gone.

This plan was not without its problems, however. Whenever I had an attack of fever and chills and felt very sick, I would resolve to take the pills faithfully to get well. Then I would feel perfectly normal between the attacks, and it was easy to forget all the pain and suffering that this disease caused. I continued to spit out the pills and dispose of them in the latrine.

Since my attacks came only every other day and I was able to function quite normally in between, I was allowed to return to my barracks to rest. I now developed a new daily routine. I received my daily ration of meal tickets but did not use them fully because of the fever attacks. I would then trade the unused meal tickets for Russian tobacco. I was also able to save enough tickets to carry back a whole loaf of bread at once.

Life at the prison headquarters here seemed completely different from what I had known. People were well clothed, and some of them wore their hair long and parted on the side, as found in civilian life. Conversation was not dominated by such subjects as food and hunger. The prisoners' basic needs were obviously being met. Although they were busy with daily tasks, they were not exhausted at the end of the day, unlike the miners, who simply needed to lie down and rest their weary bodies. People here talked about sex. They openly discussed how much they missed women and what they were going to do when they got back to Japan. My brief time with this privileged group gave me an opportunity to observe that these men's hopes and dreams were quite different from the hopes and desires of the rest of the prisoners, whose preoccupation was simply *food*.

During this time, I pulled out the Russian-English dictionary that Kako had given me and began working on the translation project at a vacant corner desk in the headquarters building. Although Kako insisted that it was not necessary for me to work on the translation until I got better, I continued to translate at a leisurely pace. It was also during this time that I finished reading *Port Arthur*, a four-hundred-page novel. I met with Pilot on his days off and continued with our English lessons.

My malarial condition persisted. Able to predict exactly when my attacks would occur, I scheduled my life around them, even climbing into my bunk just a few minutes before the fever and shaking siezed me. I covered myself with all the blankets I could gather and waited. When it hit, the entire tier of bunks shook with my body. Other members of my squad and most of those living in the same barracks were aware of my condition and did not even bother to talk to me as I lay there shaking. My lower back ached severely from the strain of shaking for two long hours. At times like this, I wondered if I should continue to throw away the pills or do what I could to try and get well. After a night's rest, however, I felt quite normal and began looking forward to a day when my health would be restored completely.

It was March 1948.

26. Indoctrination and Counterindoctrination

Although we had removed our grade insignia from our jacket collars and had technically done away with the Japanese Imperial Army ranks by the early summer of 1946, the former ranking officers were still in leadership positions in the camps. It was rather surprising for those of us from Krasnoyarsk to find that the Japanese head of the coal mine camp was a mere former sergeant in the Japanese Army. Rumor had it that, while this sergeant, Saito, was a college student in Japan, he was a leader of a radical left-wing organization. "Man, it must've been like homecoming for him when he was brought over here," the men would say sarcastically, looking over their shoulders to make sure that no one else was within hearing distance.

We were told that, when the prisoners first arrived at this camp, their leader was a lieutenant colonel. Saito (I'll call him Red), however, soon worked himself into the confidence of the Soviet commanders and had all the headquarters personnel removed to put himself and his followers into positions of authority in camp. Perhaps because of this situation, the atmosphere at the coal mine camp was quite tense. Until I arrived at the camp, I thought that there were only two distinct groups: Russian captors and Japanese captives. No matter what the relationships might have been among the prisoners, any division was merely a "family squabble," and the Russians were definitely the outsiders. It was different at the coal mine camp. I was now aware that there were some Japanese who were on the side of the Russians. I wondered if it were safe to say anything against the Russians, even when I was among the Japanese. Whom could I trust? Who might betray me? Was somebody listening? A psychological dimension was added to the hardship of our lives: that of fear and mistrust.

Before I arrived at the coal mine camp in Stalinsk, I observed that the only efforts that our captors put into influencing and indoctrinating prisoners were publishing a weekly in the Japanese language and telling the Japanese camp authorities very casually that we were not spending all the money they paid us as wages for our work at Camp 5 in Krasnoyarsk. The Russians knew how much money was paid out to the prisoners, and they kept records of the amount of goods, such as cigarettes, tobacco, and soap, being purchased by the Japanese through them. According to the Russians, there was no need to save wages for a "rainy day" because, if a man did his honest portion of work in this society, he would be taken care of when and if the need ever arose. The fact was that we bought our necessities from individual Russian coworkers directly, rather than through the camp authorities, simply because it was an easier and faster way of acquiring what we wanted. This practice, however, kept the Russian authorities in the dark as to where our money was going.

Also back at Krasnoyarsk, the Soviets did not approve of the Japanese camp authorities' method of payment, in which the wages were divided equally among all the workers in the camp, not apportioned according to output. This matter was a bone of contention among some of the prisoners who produced more but were not compensated for it. They felt that they were carrying those who were not producing their fair share. In the end, however, the Japanese camp authorities' way of dividing the money equally always won out, and they continued to give spending money even to those who were in the malnutrition unit and therefore unable to go outside the camp to work for wages.

The situation at Stalinsk was markedly different. There was

the loud slogan at the main gate, an ever-present, visible sign of their efforts to indoctrinate. The classes that we were obligated to attend on our days off were more of a psychological burden to us. Those of us who were transfers from Krasnoyarsk managed at the beginning to be at the latrine, barbershop, or some convenient place of "escape" when the classes were in session. However, the instructors of those classes, who were also Japanese and who had been to a training school at Khabarovsk, put an immediate end to our various methods of avoidance. Announcements were made prior to the beginning of class time, and no one was permitted to skip the class unless one were on "service duty." Consequently, there were men who even volunteered for "service duty" if they could make sure that the work would keep them from attending the classes.

Two of the trainers were young men who were of average height, slim, and bespectacled. They seemed rather withdrawn and shy. As we sat on our bunks and listened to the lecture, their determination to get their message across came through. There were some uncomfortable body movements among the listeners, but no one dared to snicker or ask hostile questions. Each session lasted for about an hour. Strangely, no effort was made to see how much of the lesson was actually absorbed by the "students." We were not given any tests at the end of the sessions.

After one of the sessions, Pilot and I had a brief visit. "This is your day off, too?" I asked. "Yes, but I've changed my work. I've been transferred out of the mine and now work with two other men at an auto shop. The work is easier, and, more than that, it's safer there," he said. "I hear you've come down with malaria and stay in camp these days," he continued. Looking around to make sure no one else might hear, I told him about how I had been disposing of the pills given to me to cure my malaria. "That's too bad," he said. "I know the predicament you're in. I wouldn't know what is best, either."

Pilot, too, made sure we could not be overheard and proceeded to tell me how he felt about our instructors. "I don't know how much those two believe in what they're saying. They have this easy job of sitting in a warm place and lecturing. They know it's easier than working in the mines. As long as they don't try to hurt any of us, it's their privilege to take advantage of the situation, I guess. Of course, they have to be good actors, too," he said with a smile. Then, lowering his voice even more, he whispered, "You know what they're saying, 'Be like an apple and not like a tomato,'" by which he meant that we should be red (Communist) only on the outside, not throughout. "Just to make it easier, I guess it is better to pretend that you're taking in all this Red thing, but make sure that you don't change inside." Pilot was still working on *Port Arthur*, and we agreed to get together again on his next day off.

Although we disliked the classes, we found other indoctrination efforts were rather enjoyable and attended them eagerly. The dining hall had a large stage at one end of the building where entertainment was provided in the evening once a month. Although the men who were on swing shift were unable to attend the performances, the hall was usually filled to capacity with those from the day and graveyard shifts. Most men arrived early and sat around visiting and waiting for the performance to begin.

One evening the program was billed as a special event with guests from the German prisoners' camp coming to entertain us. The hall lights were turned off except for the ones over the stage. A hush came over the audience. Red, the Japanese leader of the camp, came on stage. He was a stout man with glasses. He did not smile, although there was an air of gaiety in the hall. "I welcome you all to the program this evening," he began. "For the main attraction, we have a pantomime group from the German camp. Each of the guest performers was part of the German war machine. But now their eyes have been opened to the reality of the wrong direction in which they had been led during the war. They now realize that the system of the Great Soviet Union is the only right way that can save all working people from the terrible oppression of the bourgeoisie. Enjoy this evening that has been provided for us by our hosts, the people of our Motherland, the Soviet Union, so that you will be refreshed to go out and continue your work again tomorrow." He finally finished and walked off the stage. We received Red's flowery introduction with only polite applause.

There were Japanese folk songs and dances, followed by the inevitable skits put on by those working in the dining hall and other groups within the camp compound. The skits depicted the harsh life in defeated Japan, where the American Occupation personnel were mistreating the Japanese people, especially the young women. The German pantomime was about a train ride with two passengers boarding the train and going through all the motions of opening and eating their lunch. One of the passengers fumbled about looking for the misplaced ticket for the conductor to punch, and they both finally got off when the train arrived at their destination.

At the end of their performance, the two German men, one very tall and the other very short, came down front center stage. Standing side by side they recited in German, "The working-class people of the world give deep gratitude to the Great Soviet Union for the protection and betterment of their lives." One held out a hammer and the other raised a sickle across it. A murmur went up from the audience because the sickle was positioned upside down. Embarrassed, the German with the sickle shrugged his shoulders and corrected the position obligingly. The Japanese sitting next to me whispered, "Don't you think he did that on purpose?" I agreed and said, "Even the pair, one so tall and one so short, looks comical. They sure didn't seem to be very serious about that last act."

I once heard a Japanese prisoner tell another prisoner in a hushed voice after an indoctrination session that a prisoner at the German camp was once seen spitting on the floor after he had saluted a portrait of Stalin. I don't know whether this was a true story; perhaps the Japanese prisoner telling it was somewhat envious of the German, wishing secretly that he, too, could do such things. It appeared that no one was actively opposed to the indoctrination program. Whether it was because of being too exhausted or because of preoccupation with the thought of food and repatriation I am not sure, but in general it seemed that most of us just went along with it, keeping our thoughts about the subject mostly to ourselves. This became quite evident much later when we were finally beyond the reach of the Russian authorities on our return ship to Japan.

27. Dealing with Hunger: Forging Meal Tickets

Hagi came to my bunk one evening and began talking in a whisper. "I hear that you draw pictures well," he began. "I picked up some thin-grade paper at work in the miners' hall today. See, it's the same kind that the meal tickets are printed on. I don't know what we can do about the ink, but do you think we can forge some meal tickets?" "Yeah, that sounds possible—let's try it," I answered. "With a forged ticket, we could go through the meal line twice. The kitchen staff feeds some two thousand prisoners three times a day; they wouldn't notice it if one or two guys lined up for a second helping."

For ink, I was already thinking I could get a piece of red brick and grind it with water to produce the right color. During the day, when the rest of the group was at work, I began this new venture. I broke off a corner of the brick used to hold up the shelf we put our footwear on. "Hey! That color is pretty close to the print on the meal tickets," I said to myself, quite pleased. Using a small piece of wood as a brush, I began to print *breakfast*, *lunch*, and *supper* on pieces of paper. I showed Hagi the forged tickets when he returned from work that evening. "Very good! They're masterpieces!" he exclaimed. "I'm going to use a supper right away," he said, as he took off for the dining hall.

When he returned later that evening, which seemed like an eternity, I asked him how things went. "OK, OK. Don't worry," he replied. "No problem whatsoever. The only thing we have to be careful of is to make sure that no one else finds out about this."

The next morning, it was my turn to take the forged ticket to the dining hall. I approached the pass-through window with my "breakfast" ticket. I felt my heart throbbing. "Good morning," I said, trying to act as nonchalant as possible. The man at the window took my ticket. He turned it over in his hand. "Oh my gosh! Oh, if I could only grab it back," I thought to myself. The man turned around as if he were about to call someone else to come to the window, but there was no other worker nearby. He turned toward me. After what seemed like a very long time, he put my ticket in the tray with all the rest and gave me my meal. I took my dish and walked to the furthest corner away from the window. My hands were still trembling as I sat down next to an older man who was about to get up. "Can you eat this?" I asked him quickly. "I have malaria and don't have much appetite. Besides, rye is not my favorite food." "Sure! Thanks! Here's my empty dish. You can return it to the window," he said. I returned the dish and left the hall in a hurry. "What a close call," I thought to myself. I could hardly wait to tell Hagi about this experience.

When the group returned from work that evening, Hagi came directly to me and said with a grin, "Got my meal ticket?" "Something happened today," I began. "I almost got caught. I think the only reason I didn't was because the guy at the window was somebody I met a couple of times at headquarters when I visited some people there." "Tell me," Hagi pressed on, "when did you go to the dining hall? You gotta use our ticket when it's crowded, not when things are slow. That way they're busy and won't have time to check the tickets too closely." "I know now," I responded, "but I don't think I would like to take any more chances. Man, I could see myself on one of those posters they put up when they catch someone on counterfeit charges that says, 'THIS MAN DID NOT STEAL FOOD FROM THE MESS. HE TRIED TO PASS A COUNTERFEIT MEAL TICKET AND STEAL FOOD FROM THE PEOPLE!'

No, Hagi-san, I think we'd better not try any more." "Haven't you got any more tickets left?" Hagi persisted. "Yes, I have two more here," I replied. "Here, give them to me. You don't have to make any more, but no sense in wasting these. I'll use them. Thanks. We'll come up with something else some other time," said Hagi. He seemed quite philosophical about giving up this rather profitable undertaking after such a brief try.

28. Repatriation: The Beginning of the End of the War

It was May 1948, my third spring in Siberia. The signs of spring were just as welcome as they had been in the previous years. The frozen snow no longer covered the ground, although the evenings were quite cool. I was still a patient and required to do only a few odd jobs around the camp between my malaria attacks, which occurred irregularly and less frequently now.

The announcer entered the dining hall door and called out, "All patients are ordered to report to Barracks 3 immediately." He repeated, "All patients are ordered to report to Barracks 3 immediately!" I stood and picked up my half-finished lunch. The man sitting across from me at the table looked up at me and said, "That's good news! They are assembling all patients. That can only mean they're compiling a list of repatriates. I'm sure of it." I was trembling with anticipation. Of course, I wanted to believe it, but part of me was cautious so as not to be disappointed if it turned out to be otherwise. "Finally!" I said out loud. "Am I going home? Can you finish my lunch?" I asked the man across the table. "Hey—it's the other way around. I should be giving you my lunch as a farewell gift, but, sure, I'll take it. Thanks and good luck!" he said. I began walking toward the door before he finished what he was saying.

Barracks 3 was part of the building where the dispensary was located. The area where we assembled was the malnutrition unit, which, like the regular barracks, had bunks lined up in rows.

Some of those who got there before me were sitting on the edges of the lower bunks, while others were standing in the aisle. Kako entered the room with a Japanese doctor and two Russians, one of whom I recognized as the doctor. "The Russian staff has compiled a list of patients to be repatriated," Kako began. "Two hundred names are on this list. There are 255 of you gathered here as patients. I need not say that all of you will not be leaving in this first group. But be sure, I did say 'first group.' I am confident that the second group will be organized very soon. Even if you are not on the list that will be read now, do not be discouraged. We will all be leaving soon." "My God! I have to be on this list!" I almost said out loud as I closed my eyes and waited. No one seemed to move. Someone walking outside our barracks was heard calling out, "Hey, wait for me. I'll go to the dining hall with you," quite unaware, of course, of the tension inside the barracks. God, if we could all wait and go back together, I thought. No, not wait, but if we were all leaving for home together at this time, I corrected myself.

The Russian female doctor began reading the list. Halfway through the list I heard my name called—"Suzuki, Iwao." Expecting this, but still only half believing, I opened my eyes. People and things around me looked blurred. I walked out of the room to another section of the building where the others who had been called earlier were gathered. In sharp contrast to the tension and silence in the other room, this place was bustling with the voices of people talking and laughing. All two hundred had finally come together. I thought of the fifty-five who hadn't made it. May their turn come soon, I whispered to myself. We were then given instructions on what to do next. Kako again stood in front of us and said, "Return to your group, and inform your leader about your repatriation. Since all of you are patients and haven't been to outside work for some time, I don't think you would have any clothing and such that belong to your work, but if you do, return them to your leader. You will all be leaving this camp tomorrow at 8:00 A.M."

It was late in the afternoon when I returned to my barracks. The group had just come back from work and was getting ready to leave for the dining hall. I saw the group leader and Hagi standing together when I approached my bunk. "I'm glad for you!" they said in unison, having heard the news. "Your last hurdle is behind you now. You're almost there. Take care of yourself, and watch your health," said Hagi. We went to the dining hall and had our last meal together. The supper tasted good that evening.

The 200 men were assembled well before the designated time of 8:00 A.M. Our names were again read off. We lined up five abreast and walked out of the gate under the arch with the slogan and fluttering red pennants. The column passed Mine 2 and headed toward the spur tracks where only nine months ago on that warm September day I arrived here from Krasnoyarsk. How depressed and afraid I was then. But now, here I was, actually going home! I didn't doubt that most of the other 199 men were feeling and appreciating this change in circumstances as much as I was. As we walked toward the familiar freight cars that now came into view, I bade farewell to the coal mound, the coal trolley carts I knew so much about, and the drab-looking miners' hall building. Yes, good-bye to all this!

Suddenly I thought of the two men who were killed at this very place. Their bodies had become a part of this land so distant from their home. I could still hear the shout of my coworker, "It's a cave-in, it's a cave-in!" when the trough operator was buried under tons of coal. Then the stubborn trolley car pusher in the feeder tunnel, who insisted that he knew which cart we should use and was struck on the head by a rail and killed instantly. No, they will make no repatriation list, those poor souls. I looked up toward the high mound where the coal trolley cars reached the top and were emptied. I could only make out a small figure in the distance who was waving at us. Some of us saw him and waved back. We waited for the order to climb aboard the freight train.

The inside of the car looked quite familiar to us, this being our third train ride since we left Manchuria after Japan's surrender and our captivity. We climbed aboard and staked out what were to be our seats for the ride to Nakhodka (a seaport south of Vladivostok, port of embarkation to Japan and reportedly used by U.S. submarines during World War II). The train jerked forward. We were on our way.

As the train sped east that evening, very few of us slept. Food was, as one can well imagine, the main topic of our conversation. Some of the discussion became quite technical and detailed. In the car was a man who was rather heavyset, something quite unusual since most of the men in this group were from the malnutrition list. Fatty always spoke very deliberately and slowly. Not only did he speak of what he wanted to eat when he got back, but he went on to tell us how he expected the meal to be cooked. He would go into great detail about the preparation of the food as well as how it was to be served. I soon noticed that, whatever else we were discussing, we eventually ended up talking about food when Fatty was in on the conversation. Of course, most of us were equally guilty of this. After all, food and going home had been our main preoccupations during the last two and a half years of captivity in Siberia.

As the train continued its journey east, the nights became colder. One morning we awoke to see all the heads of the bolts along the interior wall of the freight car white with frost. "Man, it's cold!" someone said. "It's like being inside a refrigeration compartment." "Don't complain, you fool," responded Fatty. "We're all heading home, and it won't be too long before we'll be sitting by a hibachi and sipping some nice hot tea. I can put up with anything now."

During one of the stops, someone got off the train and carried in a dozen bricks. These were placed in the middle of the floor to make a square hearth. Next morning I woke up to shouts of "Hey! What's going on anyway? Where is all this smoke coming from?" "Shut up, you fool! Do you want to freeze to death?" was the retort. It was Fatty, we found out, who had built a fire on the hearth. He was the one who was supposedly going to endure any hardship on this trip. After much arguing back and forth, it was finally decided that building a fire to heat the interior of the car would not work. With no place to vent the smoke, we had to open the small windows in each corner near the ceiling, and that drew the cold outside air into the car. Giving up, Fatty said, "Well, it was a good try, anyway. I'll bet if I was cooking something on that fire, you guys up there on the upper level wouldn't complain about a little smoke in your eyes."

We arrived at our destination on the fifth day. I thought of the many days our trip into Siberia in the autumn of 1945 had taken. The sliding doors were pushed aside, and we all crowded toward the opening to look out. In the distance we saw the ocean, the very same waters that washed the shores of Japan! There were a few low warehouse-type buildings along the dock. Beyond these buildings were some more low structures.

We jumped off the train and formed a column as ordered. The column began to move. The unpaved road leading away from the pier had a slight incline. After we made a couple of turns, we came to a halt in front of a large gate. This gate, too, had an arch built over it with a slogan proclaiming the virtues of the Communist society. We passed through the gates and saw on both sides of the twenty-foot-wide path large, colorful signs loudly declaring such messages as DOWN WITH THE MARSHALL PLAN and WORKING PEOPLE AGAINST THE CAPITALISTS! The familiar red pennants were also fluttering in the breeze. There were trees and other green shrubbery growing within the compound, which made this place less drab and stark than the camps we had gotten so used to in the past few years. People were moving about as though they were in a hurry. Some were even trotting everywhere. "Hey, look! Women!" somebody ahead of me yelled as he pointed to two figures walking to the right of us and about to enter a building. We stopped in front of some tents. It was quite warm; the sun shone brightly. "It's sure hot!" the man behind me said. "What a fool you are!" said Fatty, in front of me, turning around. Looking disgusted, Fatty went on, "You complained of the cold on the train only a couple of days ago, and now, you fool, you're griping about the heat. When we get back to Japan, you'll probably complain about the food, too."

We waited for half an hour or so before a short, stout man stood in front of us. "Looks very much like Red back at the coal mine camp," I thought to myself. He was one of the men in charge of this camp. "Comrades," he began, "I welcome you to this final assembly point on your journey back to Japan. While you are waiting to board ship, you will live by all the rules and regulations of this camp. There are not many, but each of the rules was drawn up by the people of this camp. That is to say, the regulations were made by the individuals who are living here. Therefore, they are here for your benefit. Abide by them, and your stay here will be pleasant." There was a long pause, as if he was deliberately taking the time to impress on us how self-governing this place was. "How long your stay here will be, I do not know," he continued. "Even the Soviet authorities here cannot answer that question. They are just as anxious to see you back in Japan as all of you are. I need not tell you that all this delay is the sole responsibility of the Japanese government. If they would bring in two ships at a time, nay, ten or even twenty ships at a time, the government of the Soviet Union would fill them to capacity and have all of you back in Japan where you have longed to be for all these years and months. Do not dare forget this fact." He went on to explain how we would be required to do some light odd jobs during our stay. He also explained the layout of the compound and other details.

After our meal that evening, I went to the outdoor theater. This was one of the items covered by the man from the headquarters that day. "There will be some entertainment held at the outdoor theater every other night," he said. "I strongly urge each of you to attend, for I believe it is important for you

to be prepared to face reality on your return to Japan. Make no mistake about it. Japan is not the Japan you remember or think it is. It is an occupied country. You will be prisoners in your own country!"

I was rather late getting to the theater and could only find standing room in the back. The lights were dimmed, and a man came on stage. He gave a welcoming speech and emphasized the purpose of the evening, which was to prepare us for the "reality" we would face on our return to Japan. The skit was almost identical to those we saw back at the coal mine camp: a U.S. military policeman strutting across the stage; three American GIs walking into a bar, getting drunk, and leaving without paying; an American army officer taking a young Japanese girl from her boyfriend against the girl's and her family's wishes. The only difference was the professional quality that went into this production. The costumes, the stage lighting, and the acting were very impressive. There was polite applause at the end of the show.

Walking back to the tent, I overheard only two comments: "Japanese women's kimonos sure are pretty," and, "Those guys are real pros!"

The next morning after breakfast, we gathered outside the tent where we had been the day before. A man arrived from headquarters to assign jobs to us for the day. He made it clear that, since we were all patients, the work would be light and appropriate to our condition. Most of the men were given the task of picking up trash around the compound, although it seemed that the place was quite clean to begin with. I was put in a group with five others to go to the bakery next door. We were told that we could eat as much bread as we liked while in the shop but not to try to carry out any. Also, we were cautioned against eating too much. To emphasize the point, one of the bakers told us a story as an example. There was a man assigned to this work who ate two loaves of bread. After returning from work, he got thirsty and drank a lot of water. The water expanded the bread he had eaten earlier, and he literally exploded. The six of us thought it was an exaggerated story. However, I recalled the incident on the farm with Yoshida and the potatoes and decided that it would be best if I were careful.

At the bakery, where there were three ovens operating, we paired up and worked together with a Russian soldier. The Russian had a steel bar ten feet long with a bent hook at one end. When the bread was ready to come out of the oven, the small oven door was opened. We stood next to it with heavy mittens on our hands and grabbed the tray of bread that came sliding toward the opening as the Russian jerked it forward. It was an easy job.

As it was quite warm, I had my sleeves rolled up while working. Unfortunately, I missed my timing once, and the hot steel rod held by the Russian touched my left arm. I let out a yelp, and that seemed to amuse the Russian. "I'll be taking this blister back to Japan with me," I mumbled. The man with whom I was paired said, "Be careful. Did you see the man walking with crutches back at the assembly point? I understand he's been here since last year. He came here as a malnutrition case, and he fell off a truck while doing some work. They had to amputate his leg. They say he's now well enough to go home and probably will be on the next ship. We're so close now, we must be very careful and not let a serious accident happen to us." I agreed with him.

Returning from work early that afternoon, we sat outside our tent talking about the inevitable subject of when the ship was going to come in. Fatty came by and whispered in a low voice, "Did you guys hear about Yamashita-san? You know, that tall former sergeant in the Kempei-tai." (The Kempei-tai was the military police unit of the Japanese Army, which had great authority and was referred to as the "thought police" by some.) "They came after him this morning," he continued, "and they say he's at the headquarters being interrogated now. You guys heard about how he made the patient list, didn't you? While at the coal mine camp, he had some connection with one of the Russian female doctors, and she made all the arrangements for his repatriation. Once he left the camp, though, he was out from under her protective wing, and I think some guy must have squealed on him." "Gosh, it's scary," I said. "Not only scary—just put yourself in his shoes. So close to home you can almost smell the *miso-shiru*, and then get into something like this! I feel sorry for him," Fatty carried on. (*Miso-shiru* was soup made from soybean paste that was served for breakfast in Japan.)

"I would think being in the Kempei-tai would have automatically disqualified anyone from being repatriated. Gosh, that would be almost like being a spy, you know," said the man with whom I had worked at the bakery earlier that morning. "I remember hearing right after arriving in Siberia that anyone who spoke Russian was not going to be allowed to leave because they figured anyone who studied the language did so to work as counterintelligence," he continued. "I wonder who could've squealed on him," I said. "You never can tell," answered Fatty quickly. "There must be something in it for someone. Maybe a loaf of bread, even," he said with a smile. "Don't joke about it," said Hayashi, who had sat quietly throughout the conversation. "I tell you, don't trust anyone. Keep your mouth shut, and mind your own business. I think we shouldn't even be talking about this now." We all looked at Hayashi, who was pale and trembling, and then at each other. Fatty pulled out a piece of newspaper to roll a cigarette. "I hope the ship will come in soon. I want to hurry up and get out of here," he said as he lit the cigarette and took a deep puff. "I agree with you totally," I added. Fatty passed the cigarette around.

The sun was going down in the western sky. The quiet, mournful sound of a *shakuhachi* (a Japanese bamboo flute) came drifting toward us from the headquarters building.

29. Overboard with the Collaborators!

Fatty left us after finishing breakfast the next morning, saying that he was going to walk around the other tents to see if he could bum some tobacco from someone. Almost as soon as he left, he came dashing back into the tent waving both arms over his head and shouting at the top of his voice, "The ship is in! The ship is in! The messenger is going around the tents informing us to get ready to leave immediately. Oh, isn't this magnificent!" "Calm down now," Hayashi admonished him. "You'll have a heart attack if you're not careful." Hayashi had a big grin on his face like the rest of us. The messenger came through the door and made the announcement, "Gather in front of the headquarters building immediately. If there is anyone out on duty, his neighbor should grab his belongings and take them with him to the gathering place." Somehow, the man from headquarters making the announcement seemed deliberately composed, or could it be that this was not his first time bringing good news like this and therefore it was old stuff to him? As I dashed out the door past him, I thanked him in my mind for bringing the news we had been waiting for. I thought I detected a smile on his face.

There was a great commotion as men came from all directions to gather in front of the headquarters building. "Most of the people are from the groups that arrived at this assembly point before us. Man, this place is going to be empty when we all leave," said Fatty. "That's a needless worry," I said to him.

Just then, I noticed the Kempei in front of us, close to the headquarters building, standing almost a head above everyone else. "Look. I hope he's going back with us. It sure looks that way," I said to Hayashi. The man from headquarters was saying something, but I could not hear him. I was completely preoccupied by many passing thoughts. I finally heard him say, "We will now march out and proceed to the pier. You will board the gangplank as your name is read off the list." Another list, I thought to myself. Will everything be all right and my name be on the list? I tried to push out of my mind the thought of something terrible happening to interrupt my departure at this truly last moment.

We passed under the arch. I saw some of the men in line ahead of me turning their heads to give a last look, for whatever reason, at the slogan over the gate. I kept looking straight ahead as we turned the corner and began walking down the unpaved street toward the dock. The sun was bright and warm. With hardly any conversation among us, I was conscious of the sound of our heavy boots crunching on the gravel. As we turned another corner, I saw the freighter ahead, the vessel that would carry us back to our homeland! The sun reflecting on the water made it difficult to see well, but it was definitely the Japanese ship, a most welcome sight. I saw the flag with the rising sun waving gently at the stern of the freighter. The front of the column had reached the dock and stood near the gangplank. Soon we were all there.

Several Russian officers lined up on one side. The leader from the camp was also there with some of his assistants. I then noticed a man dressed in a sea captain's uniform. Must be the captain of the freighter, I thought. Seagulls were flying low around the ship. Some of them landed in the water, while one landed right on top of the mast of the ship. The assistant who had welcomed us as "comrades" only a few days ago began reading the list of names. As their names were read off, the men turned and walked toward the gangplank and climbed aboard. The Kempei was still standing in line as my name was called out.

He looked very pale. As I stepped onto the deck from the top of the gangplank, two sailors greeted me, "Thank you for all your hard work. It must have been very difficult." "The waiting was the most trying and painful," was all I could mutter as I swallowed a big lump in my throat. I thanked them for coming after us.

Once aboard, I walked over to the opposite side of the ship and stood on the deck looking out over the water. I was surprised to find so many others besides myself standing on this side of the ship. Were we that anxious to leave, or was it that we could not bear to see if someone might be left behind? "They're pulling up the gangplank," I heard someone say. After all the waiting and the tension, I was amazed at the ease with which the anchor was weighed and the ship began to pull away from the pier. It all seemed anticlimactic. "Yes, Kempei did make it," said someone.

There was one man, however, who was returned to camp. As we stood on deck watching the pier and the land grow smaller, the man next to me said, "Somehow, the Russians found out that this man had been given a message by his friend back at the camp he came from and that his plan was to swallow the paper the message was written on just before boarding ship. After he was on board, he planned to retrieve it from his stool and take it back with him to Japan." "I don't know what the message was all about, but it sounds pretty far-fetched to me. But then, it could be true," I answered. Nakhodka was almost out of sight. I found Fatty standing by me. "I wonder if somebody will ever dig my message out of the ground," he said. "What message?" I asked. "What are you talking about, anyway?" He confided, "Oh, back at the coal mine last summer, when I was still working, the conveyer machine broke down, so I dug a hole in the floor of the pit and shouted, 'You damn country, Russia!' into the hole and then covered it up." "About the only thing one could do to let his frustration out," I said, laughing with Fatty.

As the ship sailed farther out to sea, I tried to digest the reality of going home at last. It was early March three years ago when I left Hakata for Pusan, Korea. What a difference! The direction of my journey was reversed now, and so was my state of mind. I so looked forward to going home, and now that was actually going to happen!

"Hey, where is everybody?" I asked, noticing that there was no one on deck except Fatty and me. "Let's go down in the hold and see," suggested Fatty as he turned to walk toward the stairs. I followed him. The freighter had three levels below deck, with two large openings: one toward the bow of the ship and the other near the stern. These openings were for loading and unloading the freight when the ship was in regular use, but, on these voyages, they were kept open for ventilation. Fatty and I found a place to sit on the upper level where people were gathered. "What's up?" I asked no one in particular. "Thank you for gathering here." It was Kempei who was addressing the group. "I ask each of you to straighten out your clothing and sit up straight. Face east," he continued as he pointed toward the bow of the ship. "Bow deeply toward the imperial palace," he commanded. "Now let us sing our national anthem. We have been denied this privilege far too long. Let us all sing from the bottom of our hearts." The entire ship vibrated with the loud singing of the anthem, "Kimi-ga-yo."

Kempei stood up when the last word died down. "I have something very important to bring before you at this time. We have all endured many and great hardships. Most of the suffering we could accept. If the Russians were harsh, I think we were resigned to the fact that they were our conquerors, and we did our best to persevere. However! Yes, however, what we shall not forget, and what we cannot leave without taking proper action about, is that many of us suffered because of certain fellow prisoners. I shall not refer to them as 'fellow Japanese' because I do not want to stain our people's name. You are well aware of whom I am speaking. Camp leader Red and his cohorts not only took what meager food was given to us but tried to contaminate our minds with the filth of the Communist ideology. They grew fat while many of us were starving. Then, when we were weary and our bodies needed rest, they made us attend their classes, trying to wash away our *Yamato Damashii*." (By *Yamato Damashii*, Kempei meant "the spirit of Japan.")

"We have two of Red's underlings on this ship," Kempei continued. "Can we let them return to Japan with us?" he demanded. A loud "No!" roared from those gathered. "It would be to our shame if we allowed these two to return to Japan. Should we not give them their just reward?" "Yes!" the crowd yelled in unison. "If we threw them overboard, it would not be the first time such an 'accident' happened. Others like these two have met the same fate." "Throw them overboard!" someone down on the lower level shouted. "That's right. Throw them overboard," came the thundering response.

Suddenly, the captain of the ship appeared. He stood next to Kempei. "I know how you feel," he began. "Some of you have suffered much because of those who were weak among you, who gave in to the other side. But now, you're all going home. I have received five hundred of you on this ship. I am responsible for putting on land everyone who was turned over to me. Please be patient and endure that which you feel is difficult to endure. You are free to do whatever you like once you are on land, but until that time I am responsible for you, and I ask that you do not create an incident on my ship."

With that, the captain left us. The crowd kept murmuring. Kempei raised his arm as if to ask for silence. The two accused were on their knees at his feet with their heads bowed. "They're getting some of their own medicine, but it's still too bad," I thought. Kempei began speaking again, urging the crowd to get rid of the two men. The crowd responded with, "Throw them overboard!" Again, the captain came down to quiet them. When he left, Kempei raised the shouts of the crowd to a deafening crescendo. The captain returned for the third time. He made a passionate plea for the crowd to settle down. After delivering his speech to the crowd, he remained and continued to negotiate with Kempei, who stood with his arms folded and his chin in his hand. He nodded his head. They both bowed to each other. The accused men got up and walked out ahead of the captain. "I wonder what's going to happen," someone sitting behind me said. "I think the captain will keep the two someplace away from the rest of us for the duration of the trip for their safety," Fatty answered.

As I stood up and began to work my way back up onto the deck, I heard both pros and cons about the incident that had just taken place. "We should've thrown them overboard when we had the chance." "Think of those guys' families back home. How would they feel if they found out they were thrown into the ocean when they were so near home?" "I know how Kempei must feel. Remember the low profile he kept after leaving the coal mine camp? Those days must have really been difficult and scary for him. I don't blame him for trying to get revenge." I was back on deck. The cool breeze felt good on my face. The sound of the waves was pleasant music to my ears.

For our latrine, the boat was fixed with small wooden decks three feet wide and cantilevered out over both sides of the vessel. We squatted on two spaced wooden planks and held on to the railings as we answered nature's call. Sitting there in that position, I thought of the man who didn't make this ship. I wondered how he would have picked up the paper message from his stool when excrement was dropped directly into the ocean.

30. Fuji River, Imperial Valley

Unlike the trip to Pusan in 1945, the sea was calm, and we arrived at Maizuru Port in the late afternoon of the second day. Standing on the deck, I saw the sight I so longed to see. I had waited for this for almost three years. It was odd that I did not find myself terribly thrilled or excited, however. Why? I did not know, and still do not know, why my reactions to this moment were so lukewarm. Perhaps I never felt Japan was my true "home," having had all of my formative years in America, where my blood family still lived; perhaps I always controlled my emotions and never learned to express myself openly, whether the occasion in question was a sad one or a glad one. Or perhaps, after three years of not knowing if I would ever survive the Siberian exile, I was simply incredulous of this new situation and somewhat numb. I can only guess that it was a mixture of all these feelings and factors. I was glad to be back—that's for sure.

Still on the deck of the ship, I saw U.S.-built automobiles parked near the dock. "I wonder what kind of car that is," I said. "What?" barked Fatty, who could not believe what he just heard. "You fool, looking at a car and saying you wonder what kind of car it is. We're home! We're back home! Aren't you glad to be back in Japan?" "Oh, sure, I'm glad," I responded, but not in a way that satisfied Fatty.

We climbed down the gangplank and walked ashore. We formed a single-file line and went through a gate at which two people were standing. One was a man who appeared to be a Japanese government official, and I assumed he was connected with the repatriation of former soldiers. The other was a Nisei GI dressed in his khaki summer U.S. Army uniform. He wore dark sunglasses, and the small, gold-colored U.S. insignia on his collar gleamed.

We were taken to an area with long rows of tables, where we were to write our names and addresses in a ledger. All the ex-officers were ordered to go to a separate area. The names of a few ex-noncoms and soldiers were called out, as if they were picked at random, and they were ordered to go into the same building where the officers were directed to go. I wanted to go to the latrine and began wandering away from the rest, when suddenly I heard a female voice calling out to me. "Don't do that. Don't do that. You must not go away from the designated area. If you do that, *shinchugun-san* will reprimand you." (*Shinchugun-san* were the Occupation personnel.) Oh, my gosh, I said to myself. What is this anyway? Are they going to tell me to do this or not do that because everything has to be approved by the Honorable Occupation Personnel now, in place of the Russians I just left behind? So it was to be.

We were issued new clothing and shoes. They also passed out a telegram form to each of us to notify our family that we had returned. "I don't know where my family is," said Fatty. "They could still be in Tokyo if our house hasn't been bombed, or they could have evacuated to Nagano Prefecture, where my father was born. I don't know where to send my telegram." "Here, why don't you take mine and send one to each place," I said to him and gave him my form. Fatty hesitated and asked what I was going to do. I told him that it wouldn't make much difference since I would be home not much later than the telegram anyway.

The next morning we proceeded to the Maizuru Railroad Station, where we exchanged good-byes with each other and boarded trains going in different directions. The train I boarded traveled through Kyoto and headed east on the Tokaido Trunk

Line. Looking out the window, I tried to sort out a huge web of my emotions, memories of the past three years and thoughts about my future, but I was too tired and soon fell asleep.

The train pulled into Fuji Station in Shizuoka Prefecture, where I got off to transfer to the smaller local line. The local train was crowded, mostly with students going home from their school in the city. They were in their summer uniforms, the girls in white blouses and navy-blue skirts and the boys in their short-sleeved white shirts and dark trousers. They seemed to be talking, with occasional laughter, about what had happened to them at school that day. Their gaiety and liveliness was such a contrast to the bleak and depressing atmosphere of prison camp I had lived through in Siberia. Through the train window, I looked up at the soaring slopes of Mount Fuji, the mountain as magnificent as I remembered it to be.

I knew I was home.

After an hour's ride, I was at the small Ide Station, the station from which I had departed three years before to go to war. I looked down toward the Fuji River. Its clear water was still flowing peacefully, just as I remembered. My thoughts again drifted back to Imperial Valley in California and its muddy irrigation canals. I said to myself, I must send a telegram to my parents in America and let them know that I've returned safely. They'll be overjoyed!

It was 13 June 1948.

Epilogue

I walked down the hill from the railroad station to the bank of the Fuji River, where I boarded a small wooden ferryboat with two other passengers to cross the river. They were chatting with each other about the shopping trip they had gone on, completely ignoring my presence. After all, I didn't look any different from anyone else, with nothing to show that I had just returned from Siberia. I realized then how much I had become Japanese. I remembered how often I had met a curious gaze from people because of the clothes I wore and the haircut I had when I was newly arrived from America.

Paying the boatman the fare, I got off the boat onto the graveled path where, three years before, a group of children had gathered and sung to see me off to war. As I approached my village, a couple of farmers working in the field seemed to recognize me and waved. I returned their greetings with a bow and continued walking on the narrow path along the stream, crossed two bridges, and finally arrived at the gate of my house.

Hearing me call out, *Konnichiwa! Tadaima!* (Hello! I'm home!), my adoptive mother came rushing out to the entrance of the house, where I was standing. She looked as if she had seen a ghost and covered her mouth with her hand, a gesture I had seen Japanese women make when they are greatly surprised. "Oh my!" she cried out and began to sob. She called out to my grandmother and aunt in a teary voice, "Iwao is back!" They, too, greeted me with tears. I took off my shoes and went in; the tatami floor felt good to my stockinged feet. They said repeatedly, "You must've had hard times all these years. It's good to have you home safely." The glass of cold water I asked for tasted so good. Although I attempted to explain that I had given my telegram form to a fellow repatriate and, therefore, was unable to notify them of my return from Siberia, they seemed too overcome to pay any attention to what I was saying. A few neighbors were quick to find out about my return and came to greet me. It was good to be home.

On my first observation, life in the village seemed to have changed very little. Soon, however, it became apparent that people were suffering from shortages of daily necessities, particularly food, even in a farming village like ours. I was told of the period immediately after Japan's surrender when the food shortage was extreme. The villagers gathered weeds, any edible wild plants, to supplement their meager food rations, while some of their farm animals literally starved to death. Even now, three years later, food was scarce; I knew that the dream I had in Siberia of feasting on my return to Japan was going to remain just a dream. Even so, there were no more Russian captors, no watchtowers or fences, and in this mountain village not even the American Occupation personnel. The war was finally over for me. It was time to rest, and I savored it.

After my father returned from a business trip to Osaka, we sat down to talk about my future. I expressed my desire to be on my own and look for a job, perhaps with the Occupation Forces in Kofu, where I'd be able to use my English. He raised no objections to my idea, although I was not sure if he was in total agreement with me. I visited the military government in Kofu, as suggested by our family doctor, and was promptly offered a position after a brief interview. I left home to live in Kofu.

My work in the Civil Information Section involved translating articles from local newspapers that were of special interest to the Occupation personnel. I later became the interpreter for the section chief, Mr. Judge, whose goal was to visit all 201 towns and villages in Yamanashi Prefecture to make sure that they were disseminating sufficient information to the populace on such matters as voting, taxation, and the farm-product distribution system.

It was not too long before the military government of the Occupation Forces began consolidating its work by closing down the prefectural units and transferring their duties to the regional office in Tokyo, which, in the end, took total responsibility for all nine prefectures in the Kanto region. On Mr. Judge's recommendation, I applied for and got a position in the Tokyo office in the fall of 1949. Mr. William Giltner, a newspaperman from Montana, was now my section chief. Since the entire Kanto region was in our jurisdiction, we were on the road a great deal, visiting local offices in all the prefectures to promote information activities such as the development of local newspapers and the use of radio stations and other public media.

It was during this time that I met Minako Hirata, who also worked in the capacity of translator-interpreter in the same office. As we lived in the same section of Tokyo, we commuted to and from work together whenever possible. We later became engaged to be married.

Perhaps because of the distance between the two places, I rarely visited my family in Yamanashi after moving to Tokyo. Nor was there much written communication between my parents and me. In the meantime, my mother in America wrote to me often, expressing her concern about my well-being and asking if there was anything I needed from her. However, I must confess I was not a good correspondent; I did not let her know much about my life in Tokyo.

When I was still working in Yamanashi, I had visited the American consulate in Yokohama to inquire about my citizenship status, on the suggestion of Mr. Judge. I was told then that I had lost my American citizenship because I had served in the Japanese Army. This information had convinced me—for the time being at least—that I should stay in Japan permanently as a

Japanese citizen. In 1951, however, my mother in America wrote me suggesting that I return to the United States to further my education. I later heard that she regretted the decision she and my father had made many years ago to give me away to her brother in Japan and wanted to do whatever she could to give me a chance for further self-development. In spite of the fact that I had my mind made up to spend the rest of my life in Japan, her wishes moved me, and I began to hope that my return to the United States would become a reality. By then, the work of the Occupation Forces was winding down. I knew my job with them would not last long and that I would face an uncertain future without adequate education or marketable skills.

I began to prepare for my trip to America by obtaining a passport from the Ministry of Foreign Affairs. With it, I visited the American embassy to get a student visa. To my consternation, the embassy refused to issue me a visa, insisting that I was not really a Japanese citizen and, therefore, could not travel on a Japanese passport, despite the fact that the Japanese government had given me a passport. What bureaucratic nonsense! Subsequently, the embassy granted me a document called an *affidavit of identity*, a permit for me to enter the United States.

My father came out from Yamanashi to visit me when I got all the papers in order and reserved a space on a Norwegian steamship. It was a cordial visit; he approved of the idea of my going back to school in America and wished me well. I suspected he knew then that I would not be returning to Japan as his adopted son. Now, years after his death, I wish I had been a more thoughtful son to him and communicated better with him as to what I was going through in those days. I felt that my relatively short stay with my adoptive family had not given me a chance to build as close a relationship with them as everyone concerned had hoped. I did not go back to Yamanashi to say good-bye to the family.

I should point out that another factor was involved in my decision. My adoptive mother's niece, Sayoko, had also lived with the Suzuki family since her infancy, and, on reaching elementary school age, she had been legally adopted by the family. Perhaps because of her presence, I did not feel that I was abandoning the family completely by returning to the United States. She could marry a man who would take her family name to perpetuate the Suzuki line. In fact, that is what happened after I left them.

My mother, my brother Pat, Minako, who was studying in San Francisco as a foreign student at the time, and Mrs. Inaba, whom my parents had known from their village in Japan, were on hand to meet me when I arrived at a San Francisco pier on a Saturday in March 1952. I was, however, held overnight in the INS building because of what the immigration officials thought was a faulty chest X-ray photo. I was released the next day as the X-ray situation was cleared and took a train to Palo Alto to join my parents, who lived in a house they had just purchased in East Palo Alto.

My parents were overjoyed to have me back with them, and I was glad to be back in the United States. My father was impressed with my expanded Japanese vocabulary, which was, of course, inevitable, given the little Japanese that I had known when I had left thirteen years before. My father had aged a great deal, I thought, but he said he was in good health and was working as a gardener in a nearby town, Atherton. I wondered what it was like for him and the family to live here while Japan and the United States were fighting as enemies. Stories of their experiences were told to me in bits and pieces.

Two and a half months elapsed after the Japanese bombed Pearl Harbor. On 19 February 1942, Executive Order 9066 was issued, ordering the removal of all people of Japanese ancestry from the West Coast and their relocation in inland internment camps. That day, it was unusually cold in Imperial Valley, California, where my family lived. It was such a contrast to the extreme summer heat for which the region was known. What happened to my family, particularly my father, that day was as chilly an incident as the freezing temperature itself.

Three FBI agents drove up to my father's farmhouse. One of them got out of the car and came to the door as my mother was clearing the table after lunch. Towering over my mother and looking beyond her into the house as if he were searching for something, he asked, "Where is Mr. Sano?" "He in ranch," my mother replied. He stood there for a while, still looking around, then said "OK," turned around, and walked toward the car, where the other two agents were waiting. They drove out on the dirt road to the spot where my father was supervising the farm-workers. The agents walked over to him and ordered him into the car. The driver was alone in the front seat, while my father sat in the back seat between the other two agents.

The car turned around and came back to the farmhouse, where my mother was still standing outside the door. The agent who had spoken to her earlier approached her and told her to fetch a suitcase, raising his right hand and pointing one finger to make sure she understood. He said to her, "Put Mr. Sano's clothes in the suitcase and make sure you pack his warm clothes." My mother tried to explain that it would be better if her husband could come in and do the packing himself since he always took care of his own clothes. Whether the agent thought it risky to let my father go into the house or was simply following proper pro-cedure, he pointed at my mother and said, "No, you get the suit-case and pack." "They're taking him away! Where to? I wonder for how long?" Such terrifying thoughts swept across her mind as she opened the drawer where my father kept his clothes and began putting some of them in the suitcase.

In the meantime, one of the agents had entered an unlocked cabin used as a storage shed, where he had searched and taken a few items from a trunk. My father was to find out later that those items were used as "evidence" during his interrogation sessions. My father was still sitting between the two agents when my mother went out to the car with the suitcase.

As long as I can remember, my parents had a daily devotional time before they retired for the day. They would sing two hymns and read a chapter from the Bible before they each said a long prayer. As my father was about to be taken away, my parents both asked the FBI agents if they might be allowed to have a little time for prayers. The agents looked at each other, and one of them said yes. Thinking that they could pray in the house as they always did, my father moved toward the car door on the side where my mother was standing, only to be blocked by the agent, who said, "No, you must sit here. Your wife can stand where she is, and you can have your time of prayer here in the car." They felt helpless and yet were grateful for permission to pray. With my father sitting in the back seat between the two FBI agents and my mother standing outside the car, they sang a hymn, and they each offered a prayer.

The motor was started, and the car sped away. As my mother was still standing outside looking into the distance where the car had disappeared, the school bus drove up and dropped off my two sisters and brother. My sisters were thirteen and eleven years old and my brother ten. The sun was going down on the western horizon, and they all felt a chill in the air. Florence, the oldest of the three, could only say, "I'm sure everything will be all right," when my mother told them what had happened that afternoon. The four of them walked into the house in silence; with my father gone, the house felt very empty.

My father was taken to the federal penitentiary on Terminal Island near Los Angeles along with some other Japanese men in the community. In happier days, our family had spent many summer months on the island to get away from the heat of Imperial Valley. There was a large Japanese community there with a number of stores and churches, and my father easily recognized where he was taken. The stay at Terminal Island was only temporary, however, and before long my father and the other men were shipped to Bismarck, North Dakota. The captives now knew why they were told to pack warm clothes when the FBI came after them.

It was there in Bismarck that the "interviews" began. "You have a son in Japan, don't you?" was one of the questions asked early in the process. "Yes, I do," my father answered. "And he is in the military service over there, isn't he?" said the interrogator. Knowing I was not yet eighteen years old, my father answered, "No, he is not; he is too young. He is going to school." A few days later, the same questioner brought out a photo of me in my school uniform and showed it to him, saying, "Are you still going to deny that your son in Japan is in the military? What do you say about this picture?" My father could hardly believe the interrogator did not know that in Japan all students of middle-school age or older wore uniforms. He tried to explain this fact, but his explanations met deaf ears.

They also produced a cotton hand towel with a Buddhist temple logo that looked like a swastika, except the direction of the lines was reversed. This towel had been sent from Japan to my family in acknowledgment of a monetary contribution my parents had sent to help rebuild the temple located in my father's village. To this day, no one knows if this interrogator really believed that my father had something to do with a Nazi organization.

After my father was taken to Bismarck, my brother Patrick, who had been attending college in Los Angeles, returned home. It was March, and, by this time, there was news that all people of Japanese ancestry were to be evacuated from the West Coast. Our family physician, Dr. Augustus Foster, felt that life in camp would not be desirable for youngsters and made arrangements for my sister Florence to be sent to Colorado to live with a family in the church organization of which he was a part. Florence remembers that when she and three other girls arrived in Denver, there were FBI agents waiting for them at the station even before their host families arrived to meet them. The families gave the agents all the details of the arrangements that had been made and were finally allowed to take the girls home.

On 19 May 1942, three months to the day after my father was taken to North Dakota, my mother, two brothers, and a sister

were taken to Poston, Arizona, one of the ten so-called relocation camps. My father was finally released from the Bismarck
detention facility and joined the rest of the family in Poston in
the fall of that year. Florence remembers that when she was
growing up, my father often told her how fortunate she was to
live in this country, with the freedom and the opportunities to be
who she was. After the experience in Bismarck, however, he
never said it again. Perhaps the greatest loss he suffered because
of the war was not the material possessions he had to leave
behind when he was taken to camp but the hopes and dreams he
had held for America that were so cruelly dashed to naught.

My family left Poston in October 1944 for Media,
Pennsylvania, where a Quaker family took them in and gave them
shelter and my father a job until the war ended. They were then
allowed to return to California.

For a few months after I returned to the United States, I went
out with my father to help him do the gardening work and to
give myself time to adjust to life here and think about my
future. Before too long, at a suggestion of the Inabas' neighbor, who worked at the Minton Lumber Company in Mountain
View, I applied for a job at Minton's and began working in its
cabinet shop.

As I mentioned earlier, I had lost my American citizenship
because I had served in the Japanese Army. I became a citizen
again, this time by naturalization, soon after my return to
California. In 1955, I made a two-week trip to Tokyo to marry
Minako, who was then allowed to obtain permanent resident status as the "spouse of an American citizen." Three years later, she,
too, became naturalized.

My interest in architectural drawing grew as I watched my
brother Pat engaged in drafting work. With much encouragement from Minako, I enrolled in a correspondence course in
architectural drawing. When I completed the course two years
later, I was given an opportunity to transfer from the cabinet

shop to the drafting department at Minton's. Also, this training resulted in my taking on additional drafting work at home for friends and for contractors to whom I had been introduced by people who had business dealings with Minton's. I was fortunate to have the work world open up this way for me. Owens Minton, my boss, was someone with whom I enjoyed having conversations about topics that were unrelated to work. We participated together in marches and demonstrations against the Vietnam War, and he allowed me to decline to participate in the company's projects involving the military or businesses that ignored the struggles of the farmworkers. I remember Owens, who died a few years ago, with a deep sense of gratitude and admiration for his integrity and willingness to let me act on my beliefs. In 1988, I retired from Minton's after thirty-six years of service, and I continue to be happily engaged in architectural work on my own for contractors and homeowners.

In the fall of 1989, I found myself tiring easily and had little appetite, which naturally caused weight loss. Although there were no other symptoms to speak of, I visited my doctor, expecting to be told that there was nothing to worry about. A battery of tests I was given did not show anything out of the ordinary, but a gastroscopy done on the doctor's advice revealed a malignant tumor in the stomach that was "bleeding with a vengeance," as my surgeon described it. I had surgery a few days before Christmas that year, and a tumor the size of a golf ball, along with two-thirds of my stomach, was removed. For six months following the operation, I suffered from various side effects of chemo-radiation therapy, which, in a way, was far more difficult to endure than the surgery itself. Thanks to the competent and ongoing care that I received from my doctors and much support from my family and friends, the cancer is in permanent remission, and my health has been restored.

Many of our close friends are from the First Presbyterian Church of Palo Alto, where we have been active members since 1960. It is difficult to imagine what it might be like to live without the kind of care, love, and friendship we receive and give in this supportive community. It is also an active community of faith committed to causes of justice such as promoting peace, working against racism, assisting refugees, caring for the planet we live on, offering sanctuary in wartime, advocating justice for the poor and powerless, and welcoming gays and lesbians.

To say that my family is a big part of my life is an understatement. Minako and I have been married for forty years and have shared the joys of many happy occasions as well as the pain of family crises. Now retired from the public school system in Palo Alto, Minako continues to devote much time and energy to volunteer work around the church and pursues her interest in reading and music. Our son, Stephen, has stayed in the world of music, which has been his interest since his early childhood. He now enjoys teaching and conducting choral groups at Stanford University. Our daughter, Mary, an avid traveler all her life, visited many parts of the world during and after her college days and now resides in Honolulu, exploring possibilities for a future that would reflect her interest in writing and the environment.

Seventy years ago my life began in a corner of California as a son of an immigrant couple from Japan. Now, after a thirteen-year sojourn in Japan and Siberia, I live in another corner of California as a parent of two Japanese-American children. My life has come full circle. I have crossed the Pacific Ocean time and again, as related in this account and also in recent years to visit relatives. I predict that I will cross it many more times; Japan and what happens to its people will always be important to me as long as I live.